Collins　　　　　　　　　　Teach

CAMBRIDGE IGCSE™ DRAMA

Emma Hollis-Brown and Gail Deal

William Collins' dream of knowledge for all began with the publication of his first book in 1819. A self-educated mill worker, he not only enriched millions of lives, but also founded a flourishing publishing house. Today, staying true to this spirit, Collins books are packed with inspiration, innovation and practical expertise. They place you at the centre of a world of possibility and give you exactly what you need to explore it.

Collins. Freedom to teach

Published by Collins
An imprint of HarperCollins*Publishers*
The News Building
1 London Bridge Street
London SE1 9GF

Browse the complete Collins catalogue at **www.collinseducation.com**

© HarperCollins*Publishers* 2016

10 9 8 7 6

ISBN 978-0-00-814210-0

Emma Hollis-Brown and Gail Deal assert their moral rights to be identified as the authors of this work.

All rights reserved. No part of this book may be reproduced, stored in a retrieval system, or transmitted in any form or by any means, electronic, mechanical, photocopying, recording or otherwise, without the prior permission in writing of the Publisher. This book is sold subject to the conditions that it shall not, by way of trade or otherwise, be lent, re-sold, hired out or otherwise circulated without the Publisher's prior consent in any form of binding or cover other than that in which it is published and without a similar condition including this condition being imposed on the subsequent purchaser.

HarperCollins does not warrant that any website mentioned in this title will be provided uninterrupted, that any website will be error free, that defects will be corrected, or that the website or the server that makes it available are free of viruses or bugs. For full terms and conditions please refer to the site terms provided on the website.

A catalogue record for this book is available from the British Library

Publisher: **Celia Wigley**
Commissioning Editor: **Karen Jamieson**
Editor: **Hannah Dove**
Authors: **Emma Hollis-Brown** & **Gail Deal**
Copy-editor: **Hugh Hillyard-Parker**
Proof-readers: **Ros** & **Chris Davies** & **Joan Miller**
Cover designers: **Gordon MacGilp** & **Angela English**
Production controllers: **Robin Forrester** & **Niccolò de Bianchi**
Typesetter: **Hugh Hillyard-Parker**
Artwork: **Jouve India Private Limited**

Printed and bound in England

ACKNOWLEDGEMENTS

The publisher would like to thank the following for their assistance in the research for Collins Cambridge IGCSE™ Drama:

Ann Marie Cubbin, Brighton College, Dubai; Timothy Evans, The British International School, Phuket, Thailand; Robert Henson, Canggu Community School, Bali, Indonesia; Terry Nicholas, The International School of Cape Town, South Africa; James Russell, The International School of Brunei.

Every effort has been made to trace copyright holders and to obtain their permission for the use of copyright material. The publishers will gladly receive any information enabling them to rectify any error or omission at the first opportunity.

The publishers would like to thank the following for permission to reproduce copyright material:

Cover & p1 Jack.Q / Shutterstock.com; Handout 26 text extract from *Maria Marten – The Murder in the Red Barn*, adaptation of the traditional melodrama by Christopher Denys, reproduced with permission from Christoper Denys; Handout 33 © Drury Lane Theatre: Tom and Bob enjoying a theatrical treat (coloured engraving), English School, (19th century) / Private Collection / © Look and Learn / Peter Jackson Collection / Bridgeman Images

Contents

Getting the most from the book   4

Learning sequences   6

Chapter 1   Drama and theatre
1.1 What is drama?   6
1.2 What is theatre?   8

Chapter 2   Developing acting skills
2.1 Developing a convincing role   10
2.2 Getting physical   13
2.3 Using your voice   17
2.4 Developing dialogue   20
2.5 Using space and levels   23
2.6 Applying the skills   26

Chapter 3   Staging and design
3.1 What is design?   29
3.2 Exploring sets and stages   32
3.3 Exploring lighting   35
3.4 Exploring sound   38
3.5 Using props   41
3.6 Using costume and make-up   44
3.7 Applying the skills   48

Chapter 4   Devising
4.1 Responding to stimuli   51
4.2 Structuring devised work   54
4.3 Effective group work   57
4.4 Communicating meaning   59
4.5 Evaluating and responding   62
4.6 Applying the skills   65

Chapter 5   Performance
5.1 What is repertoire?   68
5.2 Interpreting the repertoire   71
5.3 Exploring monologues   74
5.4 Exploring group scripts   77
5.5 Applying the skills   80

Chapter 6   Extended scripts
6.1 Exploring a longer script   83
6.2 Responding to specific aspects of the script   86
6.3 Writing extended responses   89
6.4 Applying the skills   92

Handouts   95

Getting the most from the book

Introduction to the Cambridge IGCSE™ Drama Teacher's Guide

This guide to delivering the Cambridge IGCSE™ Drama syllabus is intended to be used alongside the corresponding Student's Book as a tool for enhancing the learning experience. A set of learning sequences, with suggested timings for each part, has been designed to enable teachers to introduce, enhance and exemplify the activities set out in the Student's Book. Each learning sequence is headed by the syllabus assessment objectives and a set of differentiated learning outcomes to enable teachers to think about shaping the activities for the needs of all students in the group. Like the Student's Book, the Teacher's Guide includes highlighting of key subject-specific terms and vocabulary, and contains references both to the reflective log tasks and the 'check your progress' statements set out in each unit of the Student's Book.

Resources used in the activities set out in the Student's Book have been enhanced with reference to additional text extracts, devising stimuli and writing frameworks that might be used. In working through the various chapters and learning sequences teachers may wish to swap in their own materials or stimuli, and there is sufficient flexibility built into the structure of activities to encourage such an approach.

Each learning sequence includes ideas for warm-up activities, as well as practical activities designed to develop and apply skills. In addition, photocopiable Handouts at the back of the book can be used to give students the opportunity to explore a topic in more detail or in a different way. The Handouts vary in content and include tables, text, flashcards, script extracts and activities. Options are given in the learning sequences, so that teachers can use their judgement to slow down or speed up, either to take more time to explore a specific element of a text or engage more deeply with a dramatic strategy, or, if students are ready to move on, to skip particular stages of an activity.

The experience of teaching drama is a very rewarding one. By engaging in the creative process of exploring text either as a director, performer or designer, students are activating their imaginations and developing a rich range of skills in communication and teamwork.

It is our hope that the activities in this Teacher's Guide will be a support and a source of inspiration for teachers in a wide range of teaching contexts, as they encourage and facilitate the learning process, thereby enabling students to build confidence, enjoy the dramatic process, and succeed in their studies.

Emma Hollis-Brown and Gail Deal

A handy list of possible resources is given in each learning sequence.

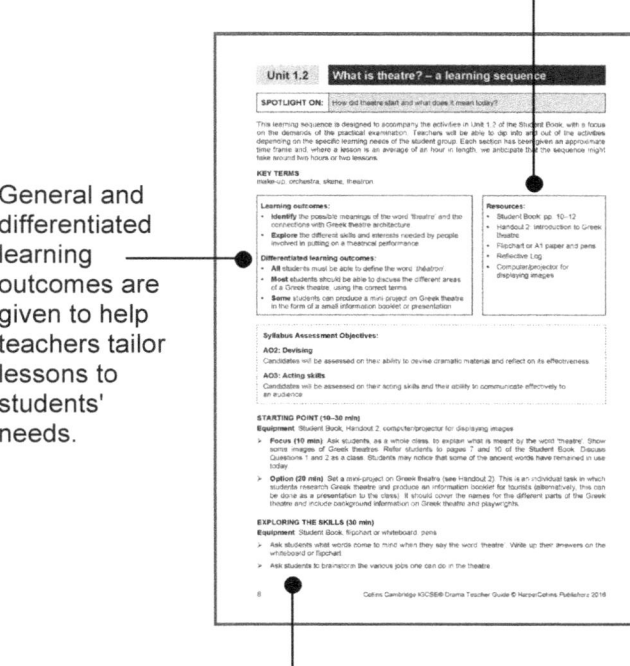

General and differentiated learning outcomes are given to help teachers tailor lessons to students' needs.

Warm-ups, activities and additional options are provided throughout to give teachers choice and develop students' knowledge and skills.

Learning sequences helpfully follow the same 'Start, Explore, Develop, Apply' structure as the Student's Book.

Useful ideas are suggested for giving extra support or providing further challenge to students.

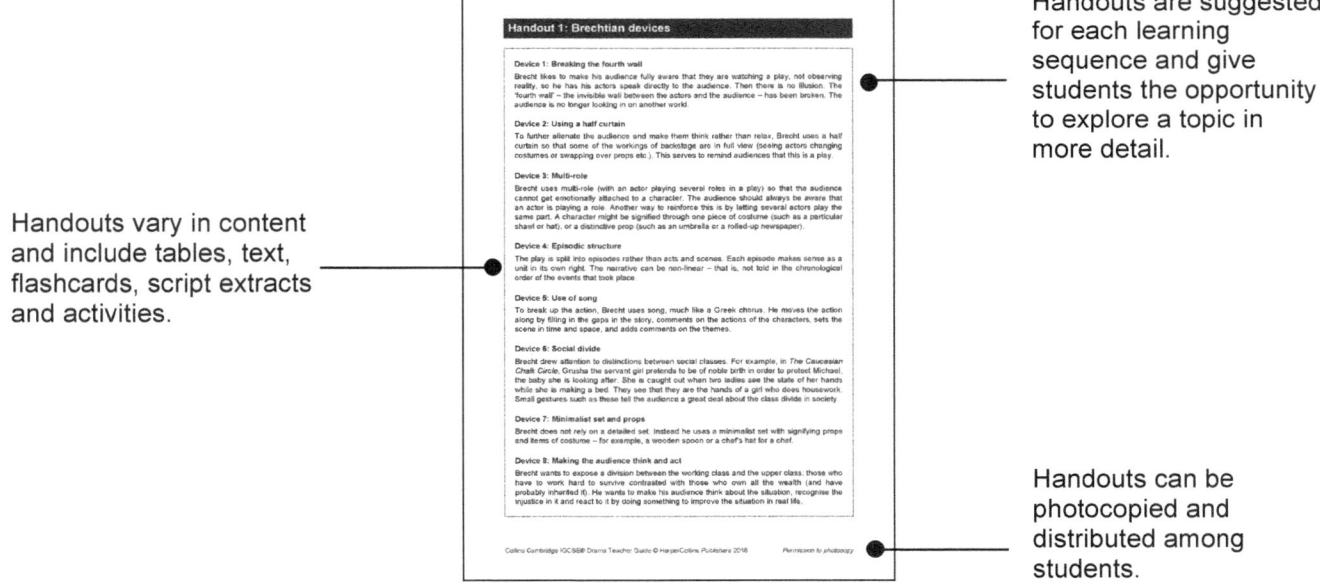

Handouts are suggested for each learning sequence and give students the opportunity to explore a topic in more detail.

Handouts vary in content and include tables, text, flashcards, script extracts and activities.

Handouts can be photocopied and distributed among students.

Collins Cambridge IGCSE™ Drama Teacher's Guide © HarperCollins Publishers 2016

Unit 1.1   What is drama? – a learning sequence

SPOTLIGHT ON:	What is the purpose of drama?

This learning sequence is designed to accompany the activities in the Student's Book, in Unit 1.1, with a focus on the demands of the practical examination. Teachers will be able to dip into and out of the activities, depending on the specific learning needs of the student group. Each section has been given an approximate time frame and, where a lesson is an average of an hour in length, we anticipate that the sequence might take up to two hours or two lessons.

KEY TERMS:
alienation, catharsis

Learning outcomes:
- **Identify** the meaning of the word 'drama'.
- **Explore** different views on what drama is for.

Differentiated learning outcomes:
- **All** students must be able to define the word 'drama'.
- **Most** students should be able to discuss the differences between Brecht's view and Aristotle's view of drama.
- **Some** students could write a short piece (approximately 200 words) explaining whether they broadly agree with Brecht or Aristotle and give examples from stage productions to justify their points.

Resources:
- Student's Book: pp. 8–9
- Handout 1: Brechtian devices
- Flipchart or A1 paper and pens
- Reflective Log
- Internet access (to show clips from TV and film dramas)

Syllabus Assessment Objectives:

AO1: Understanding repertoire

Candidates will be assessed on their ability to demonstrate knowledge and understanding of the possibilities of repertoire, and how to interpret and realise it in a live performance.

STARTING POINT (10–15 min)

Equipment: Student's Book, Reflective Log, internet access

- **Focus:** Ask students, as a whole class, to think about what is meant by the word 'drama'. Discuss the quotation from theatre director Peter Brook on page 8 of the Student's Book and ask students to what extent they agree with him. Ask students to take it in turns to walk across the stage. Ask them whether this feels different from walking into a room or down the road. Discuss Question 1 on page 8 with the students.

- **Reflective Log:** Students write their own definition of drama in their Reflective Log.

- **Option:** If you have time, encourage students to read online before the lesson about what theatre director Peter Brook has said about drama, and to think about to what extent they agree with his ideas.

EXPLORING THE SKILLS (30 min)

Equipment: Student's Book, flipchart or whiteboard, pens

- Discuss Questions 2 and 3 on page 8 of the Student's Book. Lead the discussion on what drama is for, asking students which plays they have studied and/or seen personally. Write these on a flipchart or on the whiteboard. Ask students which genre of theatre these plays represent. Make a distinction between tragedy and comedy and discuss the meanings of each. Ask students for further examples of each.

- Ask students about the structure of plays they know or have seen, and what happens in each act. For example, you could discuss exposition, status quo, problems, resolutions, denouements (the final scene of a play or film, in which all the strands of the plot are drawn together and the loose ends explained), and endings (happy or sad). Note that some of these terms will be revisited later in the course, so you can adjust the discussion to suit the knowledge and ability of the students at this stage of the course. If students are comfortable and familiar with Shakespeare, perhaps use *Romeo and Juliet* as an example of a tragedy.

- **Option**: Explain Aristotle's concept of the 'three unities'. Then ask students to consider a play they have already mentioned and see if these rules are adhered to.
  - Unity of *time*: events take place within 24 hours.
  - Unity of *action*: all characters are linked into the main plot/action.
  - Unity of *place*: all events happen in the same location, e.g. a particular city.

DEVELOPING THE SKILLS (20 min)
Equipment: Student's Book, Handout 1

- Read Aristotle's definition of tragedy on page 9 of the Student's Book. Discuss with the class whether they agree with this definition.
- Ask students to cite recent tragedies they have read about or heard about in the news. Why do these not completely fit Aristotle's definition? (The word 'imitation' gives a clue.)
- Ask students to think of a time when they were very upset about something. This might have been a reaction to a real event or to a film, play or book. Explain that they had undergone a cathartic experience. Explain the idea of purging oneself of emotion.
- Discuss with students the definition of alienation, and how an actor achieves this. Explain the concept of direct address / breaking the fourth wall and how this helps with the idea of alienation.
- Ask students to work through Student's Book Questions 4–7 in pairs or small groups. Encourage them to focus on how Brecht's view of drama differed from Aristotle's.
- **Option**: Share Handout 1 with the students. This handout explains the devices Brecht used in his work and productions. Discuss the handout with them and encourage them to do further research into Brecht, including his background and some of the plays he wrote.

APPLYING THE SKILLS (30–60 min)
Equipment: Reflective Log

- **Reflective Log**: Encourage students to personalise the content of this first unit of the book, by sharing with each other, or by writing in their Reflective Log, what they personally hope to gain from studying Drama.

Give Extra Support: to students who have seen little theatre by encouraging students to watch clips online of theatrical productions, as examples, to broaden their knowledge and understanding. **Note**: it is important that students understand that they should not describe filmic style, under the mistaken belief that it is theatrical. They should avoid assimilation of the stylistic features of moving-image drama when producing live dramatic content.

Challenge: students, in small groups, to devise a short scene showing tension between two groups of people with different levels of power (a group without power and a group with power).

CHECKING PROGRESS	Ask students to check their progress against the progress criteria on page 9 of the Student's Book and monitor their responses, making note of whether they have reached **Sound** or **Excellent** progress.

Unit 1.2 — What is theatre? – a learning sequence

SPOTLIGHT ON:	How did theatre start and what does it mean today?

This learning sequence is designed to accompany the activities in Unit 1.2 of the Student's Book, with a focus on the demands of the practical examination. Teachers will be able to dip into and out of the activities, depending on the specific learning needs of the student group. Each section has been given an approximate time frame and, where a lesson is an average of an hour in length, we anticipate that the sequence might take around two hours or two lessons.

KEY TERMS:
make-up, orchestra, skene, theatron

Learning outcomes:
- **Identify** the possible meanings of the word 'theatre' and the connections with Greek theatre architecture.
- **Explore** the different skills and interests needed by people involved in putting on a theatrical performance.

Differentiated learning outcomes:
- **All** students must be able to define the word '*théatron*'.
- **Most** students should be able to discuss the different areas of a Greek theatre, using the correct terms.
- **Some** students can produce a mini-project on Greek theatre in the form of a small information booklet or presentation.

Resources:
- Student's Book: pp. 10–12
- Handout 2: Introduction to Greek theatre
- Flipchart or A1 paper and pens
- Reflective Log
- Computer/projector for displaying images

Syllabus Assessment Objectives:

AO2: Devising
Candidates will be assessed on their ability to devise dramatic material and reflect on its effectiveness.

AO3: Acting skills
Candidates will be assessed on their acting skills and their ability to communicate effectively to an audience.

STARTING POINT (10–30 min)

Equipment: Student's Book, Handout 2, computer/projector for displaying images

- **Focus (10 min):** Ask students, as a whole class, to explain what is meant by the word 'theatre'. Show some images of Greek theatres. Refer students to pages 7 and 10 of the Student's Book. Discuss Questions 1 and 2 as a class. Students may notice that some of the ancient words have remained in use today.

- **Option (20 min):** Set a mini-project on Greek theatre (see Handout 2). This is an individual task in which students research Greek theatre and produce an information booklet for tourists (alternatively, this can be done as a presentation to the class). It should cover the names for the different parts of the Greek theatre and include background information on Greek theatre and playwrights.

EXPLORING THE SKILLS (30 min)

Equipment: Student's Book, flipchart or whiteboard, pens

- Ask students what words come to mind when they say the word 'theatre'. Write up their answers on the whiteboard or flipchart.

- Ask students to brainstorm the various jobs one can do in the theatre.

- With students working in small groups, allocate the students specific theatrical job roles and ask them come up with definitions. For example:
  - actor
  - director
  - producer
  - set designer
  - lighting designer
  - costume designer
  - sound designer
  - prop maker
  - wardrobe supervisor
  - usher
  - stage manager
  - box office sales person
  - make-up artist
  - hair stylist
  - wigmaker.
- Ask students to choose one job role and write a few sentences about what skills might be needed to do this job (Question 3 on page 11 of the Student's Book).

DEVELOPING THE SKILLS (20 min)

Equipment: Student's Book, research resources (e.g. computers)

- Ask students to research three different types of theatre building or space (anywhere in the world). Examples include: the Hollywood Bowl, California; Regent's Park Open Air Theatre, London; Minack Theatre, Cornwall, UK; National Noh Theatre, Tokyo; The Globe, London; The Amazon Theatre, Manaus, Brazil; the State Theatre, Sydney; The Winter Garden, Toronto.
- Ask students to answer Question 5 on page 11 of the Student's Book. Students should find images for each theatre and describe what is special about the location. They should think about who the audience might be for each theatre. How do these audiences differ from each other?
- For each of the three theatres, ask students to find out what is on currently and list the performances. Ask students to explain why the programmes are different for each theatre.
- Ask students to think about how a performance space might look without any seating, lighting or technical elements (such as lighting or sound). Can it still be considered a 'performance space' if it isn't a permanent theatre? Tell students they will learn more about this later in the course.

APPLYING THE SKILLS (30–60 min)

Equipment: Student's Book. Reflective Log

- **Reflective Log**: Ask students to choose one theatre job role they discussed in 'Exploring the Skills' and write a few sentences about why they might like to do this job, and how their own skills might match this job. (They could do this as a Reflective Log activity.) Encourage them to focus further on their own goals and objectives with regards to the study of drama.
- Ask the students to share their research into the three different theatres. What did they discover?
- Put students into groups of five and ask them to imagine a piece of theatre based on a story about a person being given a second chance in life. They should discuss ideas for this piece and come up with a rough plan of what it might be about and which characters play out the action. Ask them to think about the ideal theatre setting for the production, considering what factors would influence their choice. Then the group should choose one of the theatres already researched, for the opening night. Students should explain why they have chosen this particular theatre and who they think the target audience might be.

Give Extra Support: to students who cannot think of any ideas for the piece based on being given a second chance in life. Explain what this phrase means and how it might apply to someone's situation.

Challenge: groups who finish all the tasks to give more thought to the piece of theatre based on being given a second chance. Encourage them to add more detail to the story, the plot, the characters and what, if any, the implications might be for the setting for the production. (For example, will special effects be required? How big is the cast? Will a larger venue be required?)

CHECKING PROGRESS	Ask students to check their progress against the progress criteria on page 11 of the Student's Book and monitor their responses, making note of whether they have reached **Sound** or **Excellent** progress.

Unit 2.1 — Developing a convincing role – a learning sequence

SPOTLIGHT ON: How can I perform consistently and confidently in my chosen role?

This learning sequence is designed to accompany the activities in Unit 2.1 of the Student's Book, with a focus on the demands of the practical examination. Teachers will be able to dip into and out of the activities, depending on the specific learning needs of the student group. Each section has been given an approximate time frame and, where a lesson is an average of an hour in length, we anticipate that the sequence might take up to three hours or three lessons.

KEY TERMS:
body language, dialogue, empathy, hot-seating, The System

Learning outcomes:
- **Identify** the different approaches and techniques needed to create a role.
- **Explore** the aspects of characterisation and how these can be used to create character on stage.

Differentiated learning outcomes:
- **All** students must take part in activities that help create character on stage.
- **Most** students should shape and then develop their character, to communicate meaning to an audience.
- **Some** students could use vocal and physical skills to create a convincing character and perform with fluency and commitment, demonstrating sensitivity in performance.

Resources:
- Student's Book: pp. 14–17
- Handout 3: Flashcards – jobs, emotions, obstacles
- Handout 4: Hot-seating example questions
- Handout 5: Vocal skills table
- Handout 6: Character profile
- Handout 32: Introduction to Stanislavski and 'The System'
- Costume cupboard
- Flipchart or A1 paper and marker pens
- Coloured pens
- Reflective Log

Syllabus Assessment Objectives:

AO1: Understanding repertoire
Candidates will be assessed on their ability to demonstrate knowledge and understanding of the possibilities of repertoire, and how to interpret and realise it in a live performance.

AO3: Acting skills
Candidates will be assessed on their acting skills and their ability to communicate effectively to an audience.

STARTING POINT (40 min)

Equipment: Student's Book, flipchart or whiteboard and pens, Handout 3

➢ **Focus (10 min):** Ask students, working as a whole class, to do the following.

1. Identify the key aspects of characterisation, e.g. gait, posture, idiosyncratic behaviour, facial expressions, eye focus, interactions and speech.
2. Discuss two different and clearly contrasting characters, and examine how they could be played using body language and vocal skills – for example, a President or Prime Minister, and a construction worker on a construction site.

3. Using a flipchart, draw up two columns, one for each character, and write five bullet points for each outlining how the characters:
   - get dressed in the morning
   - get to work (walking, driving, being driven, running, travelling by train / tube / private jet)
   - sit
   - eat lunch
   - speak when greeting a family member or a stranger.

- **Warm-up (20–30 min)**: The following warm-up activity is designed to develop physicality. It is a mime with one scenario: the character wakes up, gets dressed, eats breakfast and goes to work, but then encounters an obstacle on the way. Choose three flashcards from Handout 3 (one job, one emotion and one obstacle). Each student should devise the material on their own, rehearse it and perform it as a mime. If the class is small (for example, eight students or fewer), then each student can perform a solo, but bigger classes can have three or four students on stage performing their mime at once. The audience has to guess the job, emotion and obstacle for each performer.

- Ask the students to think about any performances they have seen where an actor has managed very successfully to 'get under the skin' of a character (real or fictional) they are playing. Ask students to brainstorm ways in which the actor might do this, drawing on the warm-up activities they have just completed. Encourage students to discuss briefly, in groups, the issue of empathy and how readily an audience can feel empathy for a character. Do they think this becomes more challenging for the actor if the character is not a 'nice' person (for example, if they are a murderer, cheat or violent person)?

- Ask students to read through the text on page 14 of the Student's Book about how Idris Elba prepared for the role of Nelson Mandela. Discuss together what the actor had to say about preparation for the role (Questions 1 and 2).

EXPLORING THE SKILLS (30 min)

Equipment: Student's Book, Handout 5, Handout 32, Reflective Log, pens or possibly tablets

- Explain 'The System' to students, as outlined at the top of page 15 of the Student's Book. Discuss with students how far they think Stanislavski's approach can help actors to prepare.

- **Option**: Give each student a copy of Handout 32, or ask students to do some research into Stanislavski's method, before the lesson. Ask them to see if they can find examples of actors who have used The System to prepare for a role. Invite students to share their research with the class.

- Ask students to read the short dialogue on page 15 of the Student's Book, in pairs. Each pair acts out the dialogue using the body language suggested in the stage directions. If there is a trio, use both parents.

- Now change the words of the parent(s) and their body language to show that the mother or father is absolutely delighted at the news the son/daughter is giving them. Students rehearse and perform.

- Change the characters and the situation to work on vocal delivery – for example, a doctor giving a patient some bad news or some good news (see Handout 5 for examples).

- Run the new dialogues once without words to check body language and a second time with the words to check vocal skills. Let one pair watch another pair and vice versa. Ask students what they noticed about what makes a character believable and note down at least three factors.

- **Reflective Log**: Ask students to reflect on the effectiveness of different techniques for preparing for a role – including Stanislavski's System. Would they find The System an effective technique for their own preparation for a role?

DEVELOPING THE SKILLS (20 min)

Equipment: Student's Book, Handout 4, Handout 6, Reflective Log

- Ask students to look at page 16 of the Student's Book. In groups of three or four they should think about the props needed for the three characters in Question 5: a lonely millionaire, a downtrodden servant and a corrupt detective.

- **Hot-seating activity**: Give out Handout 4 on hot-seating. Discuss the importance of hot-seating as a task for developing character. How do students feel about this as a task?

- Choose a student to be 'a lonely millionaire' in the hot seat. The other students sit in a horseshoe round the hot seat. Each student thinks of a question to ask the student in the hot seat – for example, 'Where did you go on holiday this year?' The student in the hot seat answers in character, using an appropriate voice and body language. Students should try to ask 20 questions.

- Choose another student to be in the hot seat and take the role of 'a downtrodden servant', and then a third student to be 'a corrupt detective'. Some of the questions should refer to objects the character might have in their possession (e.g. a money box, a sewing kit and three mobile phones). The character can then respond, miming the prop at the same time. This should link to the previous exercise on props.
- **Reflective Log**: Ask students to write up their observations on acting and vocal skills, to show character in the hot-seating activity. Students should make notes on how useful they found hot-seating as a tool for building character. Give students Handout 6, which can be included in their Reflective Log – this handout contains a character profile/portrait checklist to help students think about character. This should serve as a springboard for characterisation and help to create a convincing role.

APPLYING THE SKILLS (60 min)
Equipment: Student's Book, Handout 6, Reflective Log

- Refer to page 17 of the Student's Book, 'Applying the skills'. In groups of two, three or four, students work through Questions 8, 9 and 10. (Allow 10 minutes for this.)
- Attempt a longer piece of improvisation with the students. Call the piece 'The interview', about someone having an interview to join a new school. Give each student a copy of Handout 6, which will help with creating a character portrait. In groups of four, students can devise character, using the handout. Students carry out the interviews, using physical and vocal skills to reveal character. Each scene should include the interviewer (the school principal who is asking the interview questions), the student being interviewed, and the parent(s). The students should take it in turns to be the interviewer (the school principal). They should try to show three very different families.
- Make notes on how each student reacts in their role to the interview questions and the personality of the principal (students can use the Reflective Log).
- Change the character of the principal each time, for example confident, overpowering or nervous. Work on physicality and vocal delivery according to the dominant personality feature – for example, for a nervous school principal, explore stuttering, mumbling, false starts and so on.
- Explore how the characters enter and sit down. Do they wait to be asked to take a seat or do they bustle in and take over the space? Proxemics should show the relationships between the parents and the son/daughter, so consider how close actors are to each other. (Proxemics is covered in more detail in Unit 2.5, but you could introduce the term here.) Focus on facial expressions to show reactions to what is being said in the dialogue, i.e. to the questions and answers given in the interview.
- **Option**: Film the performances of these improvisations and label them 'The interview'. Watch the performances on film and comment on the use of physicality (including proxemics) and vocal expression. Try watching with no sound to see how much of the character can be deduced from the body language.
- If appropriate, look in the costume cupboard and see which costumes would be appropriate for each character. Run the piece in costume.
- **Reflective Log**: Ask students to record their observations on their performances. What went well? What did they find challenging? How might they have developed character differently or better?

Give Extra Support: to those students who are reticent in the early stages of the activities (e.g. jobs, emotions, obstacles) by helping them find some simple ideas to work with. Watch them and build their confidence before letting them work on their own.

Challenge: students, using the flashcards in Handout 3, to build an improvisation with three or four characters. They might choose one obstacle and let the characters meet at that point in their journey to work. They have to work together to overcome the obstacle. They each have a different job role and emotion that defines them.

| Checking progress | Ask students to check their progress against the progress criteria on page 17 of the Student's Book and monitor their responses, making note of whether they have reached **Sound** or **Excellent** progress. |

Unit 2.2 — Getting physical – a learning sequence

SPOTLIGHT ON:	How can I use my body and movement to make my acting convincing?

This learning sequence is designed to accompany the activities in Unit 2.2 of the Student's Book, with a focus on the demands of the practical examination and the use of physicality. Teachers will be able to dip into and out of the activities, depending on the specific learning needs of the student group. Each section has been given an approximate time frame and, where a lesson is an average of an hour in length, we anticipate that the sequence might take up to three hours or three lessons.

KEY TERM:
frozen tableau

Learning outcomes:
- **Identify** what is meant by physicality, including movements and gestures.
- **Explore** the physical aspects of characterisation and how these can be used to create character on stage.

Differentiated learning outcomes:
- **All** students must take part in activities that use physicality to create character.
- **Most** students should shape their character in a physical way by working on posture, gait, movement, idiosyncratic behaviour, facial expression and eye focus. They should be able to perform in character to communicate some meaning to an audience.
- **Some** students could use physical skills to create a convincing character and perform with fluency and commitment, demonstrating sensitivity in performance.

Resources:
- Student's Book: pp. 18–21
- Handout 7: Template for physicality
- Handout 8: List of character traits
- A set of photographs
- Whiteboard and pens
- The National Theatre in London exercises on *Commedia dell'arte* with Didi Hopkins www.nationaltheatre.org.uk/backstage/commedia-dellarte
- Reflective Log

Syllabus Assessment Objectives:

AO1: Understanding repertoire

Candidates will be assessed on their ability to demonstrate knowledge and understanding of the possibilities of repertoire, and how to interpret and realise it in a live performance.

AO2: Devising

Candidates will be assessed on their ability to devise dramatic material and reflect on its effectiveness.

STARTING POINT (40 min)

Equipment: Variety of photographs, Handout 7

› **Warm-up 1 (30 min):** Select a compilation of photographs from the internet showing people in different circumstances and tableaux. Choose some in which the subjects are looking directly into the camera and others in which they are looking at another person or object. Some people might also seem to stare into the distance. As a whole-class activity, ask students to identify the key aspects of physicality seen in each photograph (e.g. gait, posture, idiosyncratic behaviour, facial expressions, eye focus and gesture). Encourage them to comment on the use of proxemics in the photographs and how this creates relationships between people.

› Give the students Handout 7, the template for physicality. The template acts as a checklist for the physicality of a character throughout the lessons. Introduce short practical tasks that can be undertaken in pairs:

1. How would the characters listed below stand, sit and move? Give each character a defining gesture.
   - An angry guard
   - A mother escaping a war zone
2. If these two characters met but did not speak, how would they look at each other? Imagine the emotions of each character – for example, scared and worried, protective of her baby (the mother); serious and defensive (the guard).
3. Show the following situations through three frozen tableaux. (Students should remember to consider how each character moves after the previous tableau.)
   - The guard not allowing the mother through the gate into the city
   - The mother with her baby begging to be let in
   - The guard looking around to make sure no one sees him letting the woman pass

➢ **Option**: For extension work, you could ask students to look at the *Complete Brecht Tool Kit* by Stephen Unwin published by Nick Hern Books (2014), pages 182 to 188 'GESTUS'.

➢ **Warm-up 2 (10 min)**: The following warm-up activity is designed to help students to develop physical skills. The teacher shouts out the instructions and corrects students where necessary.

- Walk around the space and then jog.
- Weave in and out of each other.
- Stop and stretch arms to the ceiling.
- Circle the arms eight times in a forwards direction and eight times in a backwards direction.
- Explore the space, going to each of the four corners.
- Stop in one corner and do stretches on each leg. Hold each stretch for eight counts.
- Walk, jog then stop and crouch down (eight counts each). Jump up and jog again.
- Repeat the crouch sequence four times – that is, walk, jog, stop, crouch and jump up.
- Jog in a circle; then face inwards with arms crossed in front of the body. Gallop to the side for eight counts; then change direction. Face outside the circle with arms out to the sides. Gallop for eight counts; then change direction.

EXPLORING THE SKILLS (45 min)

Equipment: Student's Book, Handout 8, digital resource for showing a video clip, filming equipment, pens or possibly tablets, flipchart or whiteboard

➢ As a whole class, discuss what is meant by a 'frozen tableau'. Read the definition on page 18 of the Student's Book together and work on Question 3. Encourage students to feel relaxed with each other so that they can be easily moulded by their partner. You may need to partner people up carefully at first, but, with practice, students should ideally be able to work with anybody in the class.

➢ In pairs, students work on frozen tableaux for the four ideas in Question 4 on page 19 of the Student's Book: Victory, Shock, Sleepy and Memory. Ask students to change partners regularly if appropriate.

➢ Discuss with students the various physical areas listed on page 19. Ask students to imagine an angry parent telling off a sulky teenager, or one of the simple situations in Question 5. In pairs, they should then create a tableau to show one of these situations. They should think about which way the actors are facing and why. Ask the students to reverse the roles and the gender. Ask them how these changes alter the body language of the actors.

➢ With students still working in pairs, ask them to show in a tableau the relationship between two best friends. Then ask them to create a second tableau showing the friends after they have had an argument. In their pairs, they should comment on the body language, facial expression, eye focus and proxemics in Tableau 1 then Tableau 2. They can feed back to the class and, together, the class can present this in the form of a table, in prose or as bullet points on the whiteboard or flipchart.

➢ **Option**: The following activity explores various family relationships in 'photographs' taken at an imaginary wedding, by considering proxemics and physicality. If possible, show a video clip of 'Flash, Bang, Wallop' from *Half a Sixpence* starring Tommy Steele (this can be found on the internet). This scene is in musical theatre style and shows a large group of people having photographs taken at a wedding. There are entertaining dance sequences in between the photographs and a song to accompany the scene. The pace is very fast, and you might use the sound track to get the group to cue themselves for each photograph.

- Ask the group to allocate roles, such as bride, groom, bride's parents, groom's parents, bridesmaids, best man and so on. Once these are decided, try to find a dominant personality trait for each character (Handout 8). The teacher could lead and be the 'photographer' in the first instance, and then hand over to a student for the second attempt.
- Some discussion of who stands where in each 'photograph' is necessary. Not all of the actors should be used in every photograph. There could be one showing the best man and the bridesmaids. He might have upset one of them and they look near to tears. His character trait might be 'insensitive'.
- The students should watch the clip once to see what it shows. They should then watch it a second time and see how many photographs are taken and where the cues are in the lyrics/music. The group should rehearse with the music three times after they have set up their 'photographs'. They must focus on their dominant character trait and try to bring it alive in performance by using body language, facial expression, eye focus, gesture and posture.
- Film the fourth performance and play it back for analysis. Students should discuss the proxemics in the photographs and what it says about the relationships between the characters.
- This scenario could be developed into a longer devised piece with short episodes all based at a wedding reception. There are many films – and even a TV series, *Don't Tell the Bride* – that could be used as resources. The wedding could take place in any country and use the traditional rituals of any culture or religion. The main point is to show all the family relationships in the photographs by considering proxemics and physicality.

DEVELOPING THE SKILLS (20 min)
Equipment: Student's Book, Reflective Log, digital resources for showing film clips

- Look together at page 20 of the Student's Book. Read the passage from *The Metamorphosis* to the class. Do Questions 6 and 7 as whole-class activities. Remind the students that a beetle cannot turn over once it is on its back. If helpful, find some images of beetles to show the class.
- **Option**: You might also show film extracts from productions of Steven Berkoff's play of *Metamorphosis* (available on the internet) and discuss how physicality is used to make us believe Gregor is a beetle.
- In trios, the students should work on creating the beetle. Share these tableaux in the class and take photos of each trio. Try different group sizes and different animals, and record the images as photos. Use film/video to record any moving tableaux.
- **Reflective Log**: Ask students to think about this activity and how they approached it. How did they feel? What did they learn?

APPLYING THE SKILLS (60 min)
Equipment: Student's Book, camera, Handout 7, Reflective Log, digital resources for showing film clips

- Give each student a card with details of a character. They must create this role and stay in character through the rest of the exercise. Examples of characters:
  - A newly qualified hairdresser doing her first haircut in a new salon. She drops the scissors and the towel. She rubs the client's head too hard when drying her hair. She pulls at the hair with the brush to unknot it, rather than using the detangler or a comb. These gestures can be worked on and then more added. The reactions of the client can create comedy, but the audience should feel the pain if the scene is played effectively. Some moments can be drawn out, such as the attempt to detangle the hair. The scenario can be changed – for example, client has curly hair rather than straight hair; the hair is very, very short; the hairdresser discovers a bald patch and quickly covers it up.
  - A retired schoolteacher who cannot stop telling people what to do and explaining even the simplest of tasks in great detail (for example, making a cup of tea). This should first be practised as a mime with careful attention paid to the size and weight of the kettle (a) when empty and (b) when full of water. The teapot, teacups, saucers, spoons, sugar tongs, sugar bowl, milk jug and plate of biscuits must all be set carefully on the table. All of these actions should be performed in mime. We do not see any of the real objects; the actor creates them for us. The retired teacher can make tea for themselves and therefore test the strength and the temperature of the tea. The second character, the person for whom the teacher is making tea, can show emotion through their face (for example, irritation, boredom, anger, offence). This character does not even like or want a cup of tea – this could be the punch line as they refuse the tea and pick up a can of fizzy drink instead, miming the pulling of the ring can.

- Make up a list of other characters, such as a neurotic parent, a busy and hard-working sibling, a lazy son or daughter, an absent-minded teacher and so on.
- Once you have established the *dramatis personae* or cast, allow students time to improvise around the character traits and scenarios. Find a way to put them together to create a short devised piece. Ask students to work in groups of four or five. The students should be able to build on the scenarios already created to make one piece. You could use the scenario in Question 9 on page 21 of the Student's Book. You could also use characters from previous scenarios (for example, the wedding photographs) and get students to develop these further.
- **Option**: Ask the students to complete a physicality template for their character. Handout 7 will be useful and students can include this in their Reflective Log.
- Students can research professional mime companies and watch mime on the internet.
- Film the performances of the improvisations in this unit, and label them e.g. 'At home' or 'At work'. Watch the performances and comment on the use of physicality (including proxemics).
- **Reflective Log**: Encourage students to record observations on their filmed performances, commenting on physicality, voice and proxemics as appropriate.

Give Extra Support: by helping students to develop their characters, using the physicality template. Give out spare templates and help students to complete them.

Challenge: the students to research the characters in *Commedia dell'arte*. Explain the distinctive physicality of four of the characters in this genre. You could use the National Theatre website as mentioned in the resource list above.

Checking progress	Ask students to check their progress against the progress criteria on page 21 of the Student's Book and monitor their responses, making note of whether they have reached **Sound** or **Excellent** progress.

Unit 2.3   Using your voice – a learning sequence

SPOTLIGHT ON:	How can I use my voice effectively in my own acting?

This learning sequence is designed to accompany the activities in Unit 2.3 of the Student's Book, with a focus on the demands of the practical examination. Teachers will be able to dip into and out of the activities, depending on the specific learning needs of the student group. Each section has been given an approximate time frame and, where a lesson is an average of an hour in length, we anticipate that the sequence might take up to two hours or two lessons.

KEY TERMS:
consonant, enunciation, pitch, syllable, onomatopoeic

Learning outcomes:
- **Identify** the different aspects of vocal expression.
- **Explore** the different ways of reading lines and apply this to a script.

Differentiated learning outcomes:
- **All** students must take part in vocal exercises and explore a range of different approaches to working with other actors to create a choral piece.
- **Most** students should be able to read the script aloud and with meaning.
- **Some** students will be able to adapt their voice in a range of ways to convey character to an audience, and create impact.

Resources:
- Student's Book: pp. 22–25
- Handout 9: Vocal expression
- Handout 10: Introduction to Shakespeare's language
- Flipchart or whiteboard
- Coloured pens
- Scissors and glue
- Reflective Log
- DVD player or computer with data projector and speakers

Syllabus Assessment Objectives:

AO1: Understanding repertoire
Candidates will be assessed on their ability to demonstrate knowledge and understanding of the possibilities of repertoire, and how to interpret and realise it in a live performance.

AO3: Acting skills
Candidates will be assessed on their acting skills and their ability to communicate effectively to an audience.

STARTING POINT (10 min)
Equipment: Student's Book

> **Warm-up (10 min):** Ask students to work in pairs (with somebody they don't know too well). One person in the pair will say three short sentences to the other (who will remain silent). The speaker should say the three sentences using different tones of voice each time (for example, excited, happy, worried, upset, relieved, agitated). After both students have said the sentences in different ways, and both have had a turn to speak, mix the pairs up so that students have a chance to work with different members of the class. After a few minutes, ask them how the different tones of the voice affected the impact of the words and the mood.

You can use these two sets of three sentences for this activity:
- I'm glad to see you. I need to tell you something. Are you paying attention?
- Oh, good, there you are. Listen to this. You won't believe it.

> Use the 'Starting point' on page 22 of the Student's Book and do Questions 1 and 2 in class. Extend the activity in the warm-up by encouraging students to experiment with the idea of emphasising different words in order to change the meaning. Ask them to use different accents to see what impact this has for the listener. They could try stuttering and hesitating to see how the audience reacts.

EXPLORING THE SKILLS (30–40 min)

Equipment: Student's Book, Handout 9, Reflective Log, glue and scissors

> Direct the students to the table on page 22 of the Student's Book and discuss the definitions given. With books closed, give each student a copy of Handout 9 on vocal expression, and ask each student to fill in definitions for each term, in their own words.

> **Option**: You could do the previous task as a matching exercise. You give the students the definitions in the right-hand column of the table on page 22 and ask them to match the definitions with the terms. You could print them out on a sheet, with the students using glue and scissors to complete the task. Do this as a class activity so they get the matches right.

> **Option**: Ask students to think about and suggest the names of famous people on television, radio or in films whose voices they enjoy listening to or who have distinctive voices. Encourage them to focus on the person's actual voice, more than the words the person says. Ask them to analyse why they like to listen to that person's voice (the pace, use of stress or pauses, the rise and fall/pitch, and so on). Invite students to share their opinions with the whole class to see whether some of the same names come up several times.

> Using the sentences from the Warm-up, ask students to work in pairs and practise saying the sentences again, this time experimenting by adding vocal sounds such as coughs, yawns, sniffs and clearing of the throat. Also encourage them to use pauses and to vary their intonation. After they have practised the sentences several times, come together as a whole class and discuss the effects these aspects had.

> **Reflective Log**: Ask students to make notes on how adjusting their voice and adding vocal sounds and pauses changed the shape, impact and even the meaning of the speech. How did they feel about these aspects as the speaker, and as the listener?

DEVELOPING THE SKILLS (30–40 min)

Equipment: Student's Book, Reflective Log, flipchart or whiteboard, digital equipment to play film clips

> Divide the class into small groups of three or four students. While working on Question 5 (page 23 of the Student's Book), encourage students really to enjoy saying the words, not to rush them. They should say them aloud, and listen carefully to how they sound and how they feel on the tongue and in the mouth and throat – for example, do the tongue or lips change position while saying the word? Circulate among the groups to help any students who struggle with enunciation. Encourage all students to take notes as they go along so they can give feedback to the class. Ask the groups to add at least five interesting-sounding words of their own to the list in Question 5.

> As a whole class, read the information in the Reflective Log at the top of page 24 of the Student's Book. Write the initial words from page 23 on a flipchart or on the whiteboard, and encourage students to give adjectives to describe the words: for example, *infection* – light and clipped; *chatter* – sharp and jumpy.

> Start a new page on the flipchart and write the list of new words from the students. Ask the class to use adjectives to describe the sounds of the new words.

> **Option**: Revise consonants and vowels. Choose some words (such as 'bottle') and ask the class to pronounce them in different accents, including the use of the glottal stop where the 'double t' in 'bottle' is not pronounced, but instead there is a very tiny stop between the two syllables of the word. Try 'kettle' with a glottal stop. Some of the speeches by Eliza Doolittle in *My Fair Lady* can be used to show how accent affects interpretation of class and, when used incorrectly, can be comic. Show extracts from the film if appropriate. If you feel your students have enough understanding of English around the world, discuss (for example) American, Australian, New Zealand, Scottish, Welsh, Irish, and South African accents, and the regional variations within those countries (for example, the difference between accents in the southern and northern states in the USA). Video clips from films can help tune students' ears into how different English accents pronounce vowels and consonants.

> **Option**: The speeches spoken by characters in plays by Oscar Wilde would be useful texts here, to demonstrate the point about the upper class in Britain in different historical eras. Try reading one of the speeches from the plays with clear enunciation of all the letters in each word; then read it while dropping the letter 'h' and the last consonants in the words, e.g. instead of 'hotel', say 'otel' and instead of 'heated' say 'ea'ed' with a un-pronounced 't' and a soft 'd' at the end. Try, in this way: 'We heated it up.'

> **Option**: Discuss with students how vowel sounds and diphthongs can vary regionally in some countries (such as the USA, UK and Australia). Discuss how actors can use these variations to let audiences know where the play is taking place or to give information about the characters (such as where they come from or what their social background is). Help students to compare, for example, the long vowel sound (/ah/)

in 'bath' as it is pronounced in the south of England with the short vowel sound (/a/) in the north of England. (**Option**: Bring students' attention to similar variations in the USA or Australia if you are familiar with those.)

- **Reflective Log**: Students should reflect on their own voice, considering their natural pace, stress, inflection and enunciation, as well as how they use pauses and vocal noises when speaking. Encourage them to make notes on what strengths they have, and on what they might want to improve or change in order to use their voice more effectively in different situations (both real and/or when acting).

APPLYING THE SKILLS (30–60 min)

Equipment: Student's Book, Handout 9, Handout 10, Reflective Log, digital equipment to play film clips

- Explain to students that Caliban is a wild creature living on a remote island in Shakespeare's play, *The Tempest*. He hates his master, Prospero, who controls him with magic powers. Ask the students to look at the photo from a production of *The Tempest*, on page 25 of the Student's Book, and to read the Caliban speech quietly on their own. Even if they don't yet understand it in full, encourage them to think about which words might be stressed and where pauses might go.

- If possible read the extract several times to the students, the first time reading it all through. Then read a line or two at a time, asking the students to repeat the lines, to build their confidence.

- Discuss where the actor would breathe in this extract, and how enjambment is used to increase the flow of the piece. (Enjambment occurs when a phrase carries over a line-break without a major pause.) Encourage students to practise saying the lines and breathing where there are commas and full stops, not necessarily at the end of lines. They can refer to Handout 9 again to help them.

- Discuss the emotions portrayed in the speech. Which words are stressed? Are there any signs of madness? Can you tell what is real and what is fantasy?

- **Option**: You could use the internet to show clips of different actors delivering Caliban's monologue. Ask the students if the actor who plays Caliban uses his voice effectively to communicate his anger and hatred clearly to the audience/viewer, even though it may be hard to understand all the words spoken. Does he insert extra vocal sounds? If so, what is the effect of this? Watch more clips from the play and analyse the way other actors in the play express themselves by adjusting their voices and also using pauses and extra vocal sounds.

- **Option**: Students could try to learn the speech and perform it in the next lesson. You could film it and encourage students to give each other constructive and helpful feedback. Each student should then write up their thoughts about their performance and about the feedback in their Reflective Log.

- **Option**: If appropriate, if you want to focus in more detail on Shakespearean language, give each student a copy of Handout 10 (Introduction to Shakespeare's language), and discuss iambic pentameter with them.

- **Reflective Log**: Give students five minutes to record observations on how different individuals have used aspects of vocal expression in the Caliban speech.

> **Give Extra Support**: by working with an identified group or sets of pairs who might struggle with the register or the vocabulary in the speeches chosen. Help them annotate with definitions of words they cannot decipher. Give them smaller extracts to work from. Remember to mix up the groups so they can learn from each other.
>
> **Challenge**: students to work in groups and learn the opening paragraph of a tragedy speech by working through it in a choral fashion. Demonstrate how this can be done. Ask them to revise what they have learned so far about using aspects of physicality and see how they can apply this knowledge to creating a choral production of the speech. Explain how lines can be learned in this way. Encourage movement, staging and gesture while delivering the lines. An individual can deliver some lines, while some words are stressed by more than one voice in unison. The more vocal variety they can use, the better.

CHECKING PROGRESS	Ask students to check their progress against the progress criteria on page 25 of the Student's Book and monitor their responses, making note of whether they have reached **Sound** or **Excellent** progress.

Unit 2.4 — Developing dialogue – a learning sequence

| **SPOTLIGHT ON:** | How can I work effectively with another actor to create meaning through dialogue? |

This learning sequence is designed to accompany the activities in Unit 2.4 of the Student's Book, with a focus on the demands of the practical examination and the use of physicality. Teachers will be able to dip into and out of the activities, depending on the specific learning needs of the student group. Each section has been given an approximate time frame and, where a lesson is an average of an hour in length, we anticipate that the sequence might take up to three hours or three lessons.

KEY TERMS:
characterisation, mannerism, nuance

Learning outcomes:
- **Explore** how dialogue contributes to characterisation.
- **Learn** how to develop a role and relationship through dialogue.

Differentiated learning outcomes:
- **All** students must take part in dialogue work and try out different approaches.
- **Most** students should be able to shape and alter the way a dialogue is performed to give a strong sense of character.
- **Some** students could be able to interpret a dialogue in a range of interesting ways, using vocal and physical skills to create meaning.

Resources:
- Student's Book: pp. 26–29
- Handout 11: Ideas for preparing scripted work
- Reflective Log
- Photocopies of the dialogue on page 29 of the Student's Book

Syllabus Assessment Objectives:

AO2: Devising
Candidates will be assessed on their ability to devise dramatic material and reflect on its effectiveness.

AO3: Acting skills
Candidates will be assessed on their acting skills and their ability to communicate effectively to an audience.

STARTING POINT (20–30 min)
Equipment: Student's Book

- **Warm-up:** Ask students to walk around the classroom or studio and, every now and again, stop and say 'Hello' to someone, who responds with the same greeting. Each time they greet someone, or reply, they should try a different tone or attitude (for example, irritated, weary, happy, excited, surprised, shocked, suspicious).

- As a whole group, read through Question 1 on page 26 of the Student's Book. Ask students to work in pairs to share their ideas about a recent conversation they heard or witnessed. Then, take brief feedback from selected individuals about their partner's experiences. You might want to ask how accurately these conversations reflect the people involved; what might they have been thinking as they spoke?

- If you feel it worthwhile, you can touch on thought-tracking here (where a group makes a frozen tableau – still image – from a conversation, and individuals speak their thoughts or feelings aloud). If appropriate, run a few of these remembered conversations as mini-dramas, with students offering the hidden thoughts behind each speaker's words.

EXPLORING THE SKILLS (30–40 min)

Equipment: Student's Book, Reflective Log

- There are a number of ways you can approach the next stage in the work, but one is to prepare two students beforehand to learn the short dialogue between Caz and Jem (on page 26 of the Student's Book) so that you can 'workshop' it with them and the class at a later stage (see below). It is important that students begin by responding to the dialogue on the page. What you are looking for here is how far they see the possible interpretations – the multitude of potential ways this scene could be played – and how much they feel that the written dialogue defines the relationship and situation in one particular way. Give students 3–4 minutes to read the script together and discuss the questions.

- Share some initial responses to the written script. Elicit ideas such as the fact that Jem has two questions and says much more than Caz – does this imply that he is more needy, looking for Caz's approbation? Or does it signify interrogation? The point of this initial exercise is to bring them to the awareness of possibilities and then to see whether in performance these possibilities stand up to scrutiny. Is it possible to make any dialogue mean anything? Or are there some possibilities that just don't work?

- Ask the students to look at Question 3 on page 27 of the Student's Book. They should swap pairs for this next task. Make sure each student is clear that Versions A to D are all subtly different. Remind them, as they read, to pay attention to which interpretations seem to work best, and which are difficult.

- Once they have had 5–6 minutes to try out the different versions, hear one of each from different pairs. Ask the class:
  - Did their vocal tones manage to convey the different dynamics of the relationship?
  - Which of the four versions did they find most difficult to read? Why?

- **Reflective Log**: Give students five minutes to write up their notes, describing what they did and what they learned from it.

DEVELOPING THE SKILLS (40–50 min)

Equipment: Student's Book, Reflective Log

- Now, introduce the different ways in which gesture can influence the interpretation of the scene, by asking the two students who learned the dialogue before the class began to perform it for everyone. Then, tell one of them (perhaps Jem) to lay their hand on Caz's shoulder at a particular point. Ask the class: how does it change the meaning of the dialogue? Does it matter when (at what point) the hand is placed? Does it matter who places a hand on the other's shoulder?

- Volunteers could come out, to replace 'Jem' or 'Caz', and try placing the hand at different points in the dialogue.

- Now, in their pairs, give students 15 minutes to try out some of the suggested gestures or movements from the list on page 28 of the Student's Book (Question 4). Then show a selection to the class, asking them to comment on how it changes the meaning of the scene. It would help if they have notebooks to hand, to jot down any observations they have.

- **Reflective Log**: Give students five minutes to write up observations, describing what they did and what they learned from it.

> **Challenge**: the students by introducing a chair into the dialogue and insist that Caz and Jem must both use the chair at least once. Then try increasing the use of the chair – so that they have to sit on it twice, three times, four times, etc. At what point – if any – does it become comic? Can the chair be used in another way – touched, leant on, stroked? What impact does that have?

APPLYING THE SKILLS (40 min)

Equipment: Student's Book, photocopies of the dialogue on page 29 of the Student's Book, Handout 11

- Ask two students to read aloud the dialogue from *Sparkleshark* on page 29 of the Student's Book to the rest of the class. Then ask students to complete Question 5, annotating the dialogue on a photocopy of the text.

- Students should feed back to Question 5 with the class as a whole, and then in pairs begin to prepare the scene to perform.

- **Option**: if you have time, you may wish to display or run through Handout 11, as a useful guide for how to go about preparing scripted work.
- Once students have rehearsed the dialogue, ask them to perform several of the performances to the class as a whole and invite comment on how the dialogues differ, if at all.

> **Give Extra Support:** by working with a group of students or sets of pairs who might struggle and 'workshop' it with them, using a pair of students as the model for the others to work with. Once the students have seen some possibilities, they can go away and try it for themselves.
>
> **Challenge:** students to prepare a variety of more challenging dialogues, considering characterisation, mannerism and nuance.

Checking progress	Ask students to check their progress against the progress criteria on page 29 of the Student's Book and monitor their responses, making note of whether they have reached **Sound** or **Excellent** progress.

Unit 2.5 — Using space and levels – a learning sequence

| SPOTLIGHT ON: | How can I use space and levels effectively when I am acting? |

This learning sequence is designed to accompany the activities in Unit 2.5 of the Student's Book, with a focus on the demands of the practical examination. Teachers will be able to dip into and out of the activities, depending on the specific learning needs of the student group. Each section has been given an approximate time frame and, where a lesson is an average of an hour in length, we anticipate that the sequence might take up to three hours or three lessons.

KEY TERMS:
performance space, tableaux, levels, staging, blocking, sightlines, terminology for areas on the stage, rostrum

Learning outcomes:
- **Identify** the possibilities of different types of performance space.
- **Explore** the different types of space (intimate, personal, social and public) and apply them in acting.

Differentiated learning outcomes:
- **All** students must take part in working on the use of proxemics in their performance work and explore a range of different approaches to working with other actors to create meaning.
- **Most** students should shape and alter the way a scene is staged in the space, using levels to communicate meaning to an audience.
- **Some** students could command the performance space and use distances between them and other actors to create clear relationships between characters.

Resources:
- Student's Book: pp. 30–33
- Handout 12: Ideas for exploring proxemics
- Flipchart and pens
- Video camera
- Reflective Log

Syllabus Assessment Objectives:

AO1: Understanding repertoire
Candidates will be assessed on their ability to demonstrate knowledge and understanding of the possibilities of repertoire, and how to interpret and realise it in a live performance.

AO2: Devising
Candidates will be assessed on their ability to devise dramatic material and reflect on its effectiveness.

AO3: Acting skills
Candidates will be assessed on their acting skills and their ability to communicate effectively to an audience.

STARTING POINT (40 min)
Equipment: Student's Book

➢ **Focus (20 min)**: Show stills from a variety of plays and ask students to comment on how actors are placed on stage. The students should consider the following:
- Are the actors sitting, lying or standing?
- How close or far apart are they?
- Which way is their eye-focus directed?
- Is their face exposed or covered?

- Are they touching or holding another actor in any way?
- Can any other particular groupings be detected on stage?
- What conclusions can be drawn from the answers to the above questions about the relationships of the characters?

Refer students to the definition of proxemics on page 30 of the Student's Book.

> **Warm-up (20 min)**: Ask the students to work in groups of approximately 6–8 and place themselves in different poses that resemble a family portrait. They should imagine that they are having a family photograph taken at a professional photographer's studio.

They could play around with the idea of photographs from the 19th century, where the women are often seated with the men standing behind, and the children either sitting in front of the women or resting on the mother's lap, depending on their age.

Students should try three or four different poses. Then, in turn, each group should perform their tableaux to the rest of the class. The class should use the bullet points above to discuss each tableau and how proxemics are used. If necessary, refer students to the definition of proxemics on page 30 of the Student's Book.

> Now discuss with the students the relationships between actors on stage and how these can be conveyed by the stage 'picture'.

- Show the students page 30 in the Student's Book and, as a class, consider the painting *And when did you last see your father?* by William Frederick Yeames, which is set during the English Civil War. In the painting, the young boy from a Royalist family (supporters of King Charles I) is being questioned by Roundhead opponents about where his father is. If the boy gives any information away to his interrogator, his father will be captured and executed. The contrast is clear between the innocence of the children and the evil intent of their adult questioners.
- A group of students in the class should reproduce the staging of the characters in the painting. Then, as a whole class, answer the questions in Question 1 on page 31.

> **Option**: Show some photographs of productions. These might be of past productions at your school or professional productions. Ask the students to try to work out the relationships between the characters either by role (e.g. mother and son) or by nature (e.g. warm and affectionate). Ask students to write notes on the photographs, using the questions in Question 1.

EXPLORING THE SKILLS (30 min)
Equipment: Student's Book, camera, Reflective Log

> In pairs, students should stand opposite each other, about 2 metres apart, and alternate saying 'Hello' or 'How are you feeling?' to each other. Each time one student says it, they move a step closer towards the other. The students stop when one or the other feels uncomfortable with the closeness. This should be at the point where personal body space is being invaded. Relate this to the diagram on page 31 of the Student's Book.

> Students work on the scenarios in Question 5, to create tableaux (red carpet movie premiere; exam results day; the break-up). They need to consider the arrangement of all the characters in the scene, in relation to each other, and which way they face in each tableau. How close do the different characters sit or stand?

> For further practice, students can also create tableaux for each of these situations:
- a wedding reception
- a court room scene
- a person grabbing someone's wallet and phone, in a busy street
- a catwalk fashion show with a full audience.

> **Option – Reflective Log**: Students could take photographs of some of their tableaux and then make notes in their Reflective Logs on how they used proxemics to show the nature of the relationships between the characters in the different tableaux.

DEVELOPING THE SKILLS (20 min)

Equipment: Student's Book, Reflective Log

- Introduce and discuss how levels can be created in different ways on stage. Look at the examples given at the top of page 32 of the Student's Book, describing what the actor can do, such as lie on the floor, sit or stand. Some other actors can even lift each other.
- Discuss the importance of physical stage features, such as rostra and other parts of the set, and discuss how they can be used to vary the levels. Read and discuss the reasons given on page 32 for the use of different levels. Ask the students to think of other examples of how different levels might be used by actors and for what reason.
- Read the extract from *Sand Burial* on page 32 of the Student's Book.
- Ask the students to work through Questions 7 and 8 on page 33.
- **Reflective Log**: Give students five minutes to write up observations. What did I do and why did I do it?

APPLYING THE SKILLS (30–60 min)

Equipment: Student's Book, Handout 12, camera or tablet computer for filming

- Using Handout 12, read the scenario given in task 1 and quickly run through the steps in thinking about proxemics and levels in scenarios. Ask the students to recap what they have learned so far about different proxemics, coupled with physicality, to denote relationships between characters.
- Work through the various stages in tasks 2 to 7 in Handout 12. Once the scenario has been rehearsed, ask the groups to perform it, one group at a time. Make sure that each tableau in the piece is held for three or four beats so it is clear to the audience. Demonstrate how to use counts or beats to cue action and speech. Emphasise the need for smooth transitions.
- **Option**: Film the performances so students can evaluate their work and write notes in their Reflective Logs.
- **Option**: Ask the students to start working though the suggested scenarios in task 8 of Handout 12 in the same way. Explain that it is better to spend time on one scenario and make it convincing, rather than rush through trying to complete all of them.
- **Reflective Log**: Give students 10 minutes to record observations.

Give Extra Support: by helping students to understand the distances that represent intimate, personal and social situations, by using a tape measure.

Challenge: students by asking them to research E.T. Hall and his theory of proxemics. They could design a poster to show the different distances between actors on stage and how these might affect relationships, using photographs as illustration. The poster might take the form of a short storyboard, with the students adding captions to each frame explaining the meaning in a brief manner, e.g. 'The prisoner tries to escape'.

CHECKING PROGRESS	Ask students to read over the notes they made in their reflective journals and then evaluate their own understanding of proxemics, space and levels. Run a five-minute recap of how space and levels can create meaning on stage.

Unit 2.6 Applying the skills – a learning sequence

SPOTLIGHT ON: How can I demonstrate my acting skills to their best effect?

This learning sequence is designed to accompany the activities in Unit 2.6 of the Student's Book, with a focus on the demands of the practical examination. Teachers will be able to dip into and out of the activities, depending on the specific learning needs of the student group. Each section has been given an approximate time frame and, where a lesson is an average of an hour in length, we anticipate that the sequence might take up to three hours or three lessons.

Learning outcomes:

- **Identify** the key aspects of a character in relation to vocal expression and physicality; identify what is happening between characters in a given piece of dialogue.
- **Explore** the different proxemics that could be used to show the relationship between the characters and how it might change throughout the dialogue.

Differentiated learning outcomes:

- **All** students must take part in working on the use of proxemics, vocal expression and physicality in their performance work and explore a range of different approaches to working with other actors to create meaning.
- **Most** students should shape and alter the way a scene is staged in the space, using levels, physicality and vocal expression to communicate meaning to an audience.
- **Some** students could engage the audience by creating characters and relationships, using a consistently powerful vocal expression and a clearly defined physicality. Transitions would always be smooth, and the performance space and levels would be used successfully, to create a clear meaning that comes naturally from the text.

Resources:

- Student's Book: pp. 34–39
- Handout 13: Vocal and physical warm-ups
- Previous handouts from the rest of the units in this chapter
- Reflective Log
- Flipchart or whiteboard and pens
- Copies of monologues for students to work on (for example, from *Twelfth Night*, *Bouncers* or *Shakers*)

Syllabus Assessment Objectives:

AO1: Understanding repertoire

Candidates will be assessed on their ability to demonstrate knowledge and understanding of the possibilities of repertoire, and how to interpret and realise it in a live performance.

AO2: Devising

Candidates will be assessed on their ability to devise dramatic material and reflect on its effectiveness.

AO3: Acting skills

Candidates will be assessed on their acting skills and their ability to communicate effectively to an audience.

STARTING POINT (50 min)

Equipment: Student's Book, Handout 13, Reflective Log

➢ **Focus (30 min)**: Ask the students what is meant by the following terms and, for each term, ask for an example of how it might be used in performance:

- aspects of physicality
- aspects of vocal expression
- proxemics (intimate, personal, social, public)
- performance spaces
- sightlines
- dialogue.

If you wanted to develop their written answer technique, this could take the form of a review test with short-answer questions. You might use a text they are studying as the basis of the questions. Whether for a test or a discussion, your questions should test students' knowledge and understanding of all these key aspects of drama.

➢ **Warm-up (20 min)**: See Handout 13 for this set of vocal and physical warm-ups. For the vocal warm-ups, it is important that students stand in a neutral position, with feet parallel, legs slightly apart, arms by their sides and shoulders relaxed. Encourage them to clear their minds of distracting thoughts and 'be in the present'. Work through the exercise on Handout 13 with the students.

➢ Working from Question 1 on page 34 of the Student's Book, recap with the students which skills have been covered in the previous sections of the chapter. Explain that these skills will now be applied to text-based and devised work. Students should refer to their Reflective Logs and handouts to help them recall and consolidate what they have learned.

➢ Ask students to work in pairs to improvise a quick conversation between Caliban and Prospero from *The Tempest*, as outlined in Question 2 on page 34 of the Student's Book. Encourage the students to think about all they have learned in this chapter, in terms of using their voice, developing character and understanding proxemics.

EXPLORING THE SKILLS (60 min)

Equipment: Student's Book, flipchart or whiteboard, pens

➢ Refer students to page 35 of the Student's Book. Read together the background information about Ira, from *Red Velvet*, by Lolita Chakrabarti. The photograph shows a performance of the play.

➢ Students should pair up and read aloud the dialogue between Ira and Margaret on pages 36 and 37 of the Student's Book. After they have finished, ask them to do the following:

- Read the dialogue again in small sections, paying careful attention to the non-fluency features, such as the use of ellipsis (…), repetitions, interruptions, unfinished sentences and fillers such as 'erm'. Students should look carefully at these and discuss them, trying to analyse their effect and impact, and to interpret any implied meanings.
- Encourage students to consider the possible social class of the characters and what they do for a living. How might this affect their speech?
- Students should consider all aspects of the vocal expression. Where might it speed up and slow down? Where are the pauses? What is the intonation for each line? How does tone or pitch change? What is the direction of the vocal delivery for each character?

➢ Students should spend 10–15 minutes interpreting the text and suggesting how to use proxemics and physicality. How would the differences between masculine and feminine posture and movement be shown? Students should observe how emotions change throughout the dialogue and discuss how physicality and proxemics would be adjusted accordingly – for example, do the characters touch each other? Students should take notes and try out the ideas.

➢ Finish up this section by working quickly through Questions 3 and 4 on page 37 of the Student's Book. You could do this as a whole class, and write ideas up on a flipchart or whiteboard.

DEVELOPING THE SKILLS (40 min)

Equipment: Student's Book, copies of monologues for students to work on (for example, from *Twelfth Night*, *Bouncers* or *Shakers*)

➢ For Question 5 on page 38 of the Student's Book, students should either work on the Ira and Margaret dialogue on pages 36 and 37, or you could give them a choice of monologues to work on. If you give them a monologue, it would be good if these could be given out before class. It would be helpful if students have studied it beforehand but, if they have not, give a brief background and explain the context of the monologue.

- A suitable choice might be Viola's speech from *Twelfth Night* (Act 2 Scene 2: 'I left no ring with her'). Explain to students that here Viola is speaking about how Olivia may have fallen in love with her. (Viola is dressed as a man.) 'Fortune forbid my outside have not charmed her.' Viola is in love with Duke Orsino and he is in love with Olivia. The duke sent Viola to woo Olivia on his behalf. Students should work through the lines to find their meaning and to see how Viola at first questions why the ring has been sent to her and then gradually realises what has happened.
- A less challenging monologue could be found in a John Godber play, for example *Bouncers* or *Shakers*. *Bouncers* has four monologues by Lucky Eric, and *Shakers* has a monologue by each of the four waitresses.

➢ The students should annotate the extract they are working on, adding gestures, movements and facial expressions as well as notes on vocal expression. The punctuation marks can help to decipher the tone, pace and rhythm of the delivery.

➢ Students should refer to Question 5 on page 38 of the Student's Book to help them.

APPLYING THE SKILLS (20 min)

Equipment: Student's Book, Reflective Log, internet video clips of performances

➢ Using a dialogue or group scene from a play (either the one on pages 35–37 of the Student's Book or another one), students should apply the skills they have learned so far and rehearse the extract. Students should work through the extract with their partners and focus on the meaning of the lines, annotating it and asking questions where the lines seem unclear. Students could look at different performances of the scene (e.g. Frantic Assembly's version of *Othello*, which is set around a pool table in a pub or bar), and make notes on how roles are acted, how lines are delivered and physicality used.

➢ Once students have had some rehearsal time, ask them to perform their script extracts or monologues for the class. Encourage them to critique each other's performances constructively.

➢ **Reflective Log**: Give students 10 minutes to record observations about their performance. What decisions did they make and why? How effective were those decisions when it came to the performance?

Give Extra Support: by helping those students who find learning lines very difficult. Work through the monologue from *Twelfth Night* demonstrating different line-learning techniques, such as breaking up the text into sections and, within each section, highlighting two or three key words and then visualising these words – that is, seeing the nouns, such as 'ring', in your head. Another method is to say the first line several times until it has been learned perfectly and then add on the next line and repeat lines one and two together until they have been learned. Then add line three in the same way. Some students will benefit from changing the size and style of the font or the colour of the paper it is printed on. They could use double spacing or cut the speech into sections and put the sections on separate pages. They could try walking around while saying the lines, or pinning difficult sections up on the wall or bathroom mirror!

Challenge: a group of students who learn lines easily by giving them a whole scene to work on, rather than just a monologue or dialogue. They can then work on all the aspects of performance and direction.

CHECKING PROGRESS	Ask students to check their progress against the progress criteria on page 39 of the Student's Book and monitor their responses, making note of whether they have reached **Sound** or **Excellent** progress.

Unit 3.1 What is design? – a learning sequence

| SPOTLIGHT ON: | How does design communicate to an audience? |

This learning sequence is designed to accompany the activities in Unit 3.1 of the Student's Book, with a focus on the demands of the practical examination. Teachers will be able to dip into and out of the activities, depending on the specific learning needs of the student group. Each section has been given an approximate time frame and, where a lesson is an average of an hour in length, we anticipate that the sequence might take up to three hours or three lessons.

KEY TERM:
directorial concept

Learning outcomes:
- **Identify** the different aspects of design, including the notion of communication, impact and symbolism.
- **Explore** the different ways sound, lighting, props and costume can enhance a director's concept and communicate the meaning of a piece of theatre.

Differentiated learning outcomes:
- **All** students must explore the role of a designer for a play.
- **Most** students should be able to suggest ways to use set, lighting, sound, costume, make-up and props in a given scene.
- **Some** students will be able to produce a sophisticated design concept for a short piece of theatre.

Resources:
- Student's Book: pp. 41–45
- Handout 14: Mind map template
- Flipchart or computer/projector
- Coloured pens
- Reflective Log
- Optional: a copy of the novel *Great Expectations* by Charles Dickens

Syllabus Assessment Objectives:

AO1: Understanding repertoire
Candidates will be assessed on their ability to demonstrate knowledge and understanding of the possibilities of repertoire, and how to interpret and realise it in a live performance.

AO2: Devising
Candidates will be assessed on their ability to devise dramatic material and reflect on its effectiveness.

STARTING POINT (30 min)
Equipment: Student's Book

> **Focus (10 min):** Use the photograph on page 41 of the Student's Book and discuss the visual design elements used.
>   - How does the set blend in with the costume and vice versa?
>   - Why is there so much blue?
>   - Are all the characters in period costume?
>   - Which character's costume stands out and in what way?
>   - What might his role in the play be?
>   - Do you think he is a central character or not?
>   - In what historical era do you think the play is set?

> **Warm-up (20 min):** Ask the students to stand in the middle of the performance space and, in a huddle, move to one corner of the space, staying there for five beats (count this out for them) then move to the opposite corner of the space. They should repeat this, imagining that they are prisoners chained together and that is why they have to move together. Ask them to consider how the stage should be lit – for example, could there be moments when some faces are highlighted, making them stand out from the

crowd. Discuss the direction actors should face in a given performance space, such as the proscenium arch. Ask the students to consider what kind of set the piece might have, when and where it would be set, and what the actors would be wearing. Could sound effects enhance the action?

- Now change the scenario and ask the students to sit in a circle in one corner of the performance space, and imagine a large, deep forest. Two students play the role of two friends who are on a camping or school trip and have got lost. They improvise the opening of the scene when they first realise they are lost and cannot get back to the group or the camp. After the short improvisation, two other students play the role of the lost friends. Then the group should discuss the types of lighting needed to set the scene, for example, the warm colours and perhaps some gobos. They should imagine the performance space is in-the-round (that is, with audience on all sides). Discuss with the students how this might affect the lighting design and the set design. What naturalistic sounds might be used on a sound track?

- Now ask the students to work in groups of three or four and imagine they are mountain climbing and there is an avalanche. Some survive and are rescued. Discuss the lighting colours and effects before, during and after the avalanche. What sound effects might be used? How could these be mixed with the actors' voices?

EXPLORING THE SKILLS (30 min)

Equipment: Student's Book, computer/projector, flipchart or whiteboard, pens

- Discuss as a whole class what importance they feel design has on the overall effect of a performance. Encourage students to give specific references to plays they have seen or know about in which the design has had a strong impact. Option: ask students to bring in images they have found, taken from plays where the design is very striking and impactful, to share with the class.

- Look at the short extract from *The House of Bernarda Alba* by Federico García Lorca, on page 42 of the Student's Book and the photograph at the top of page 43. Read the extract out in class with students taking the four parts. In a class discussion, work through the following questions, noting the answers on the flipchart or whiteboard.
    - What might the colour green represent?
    - How does this colour go against the idea of death?
    - What does it say about the character in the green dress in the photograph?
    - In this play, the stage directions tell the director what colour to use but imagine if the colour of the dress had been red. What can red signify, and how could this change the interpretation?

- Now look again at Questions 2 and 3 on page 42 of the Student's Book.

- Explain to students that the play is set in Spain, the country of flamenco. Imagine the play is set in Africa. How might this change the use of colour in the set and costume?

- Ask students to work in pairs and imagine other colours for the fan and the dress that could have other possible interpretations. They should then feed back their ideas to the class.

- Find photographs on the internet from other productions of this play and discuss with the students how set and costume have been used in different ways. Show the images on a screen, using a projector.

DEVELOPING THE SKILLS (50 min)

Equipment: Student's Book, Handout 14, Reflective Log, internet access, flipchart or whiteboard, pens, copy of the novel *Great Expectations* by Charles Dickens

- Discuss the meaning of 'directorial concept' on page 43 of the Student's Book. Ask students for ideas about what a director's role entails and what is meant by 'concept' in this context. Use a flipchart or whiteboard to record ideas in a mind map format (use the template in Handout 14, if appropriate).

- Look with the students at the photograph taken from a production of *Great Expectations* by Charles Dickens, on page 43 of the Student's Book. Students should discuss Questions 4 and 5 in pairs. If possible, try staging this Christmas dinner scene and using the idea of the slanted table. Do this in groups so that students can take part in the tableau and watch others stage it.

- Ask students to look at the photograph of the large fireplace on page 44 of the Student's Book and answer Questions 6 and 7. Students should do this as an individual task and write their answers in their Reflective Logs.

- **Option**: Look with the students at the passage in Chapter 11 of the novel *Great Expectations*, describing the room in Miss Havisham's house with the table set out for her wedding feast. Ask students to come up with ideas for staging this scene. Use the idea of seeing everything through Pip's eyes.
- Ask students to research different productions of *Great Expectations* and make notes on what the director's concept might be for each one. The National Theatre website has video clips from productions and interviews with designers and directors.
- Try looking at podcasts from productions of *War Horse* and *The Curious Incident of the Dog in the Night Time*. Ask students to identify the director's concept for each performance.
- **Option**: Alternatively, look at theatre companies e.g. Frantic Assembly, who produce lots of resources, and explain their design concepts. Frantic have produced a resource pack on *Lovesong* by Abi Morgan.
- **Option**: Ask students to read about the Little Red Riding Hood design ideas on page 44 of the Student's Book. They should carefully study the table that outlines the key design ideas. Ask students to discuss Questions 8 and 9 on page 45 in small groups. Encourage them to comment on the design ideas and whether they would have planned the design differently.

APPLYING THE SKILLS (2 × 40 min)

Equipment: Student's Book, Handout 14, Reflective Log, flipchart or whiteboard, pens

- As a whole class, draw up a list of fairy tales that are known to the students, and write these on the flipchart. You might look at the works of the Brothers Grimm and Hans Christian Anderson for inspiration. If you want to start with shorter texts, use Aesop's Fables.
- In pairs or small groups, students work through Questions 10 and 11 on page 45 of the Student's Book. They must make sure they have a clear directorial concept for their production. For example, they could use the fable of 'The Hare and the Tortoise', setting it in a modern-day office with the two animals re-imagined as two human characters. One is very fast and highly confident but gets distracted or over-tired, whereas the other is slow but gets there in the end, always completing the tasks. Once the group has a concept, they should draw up a table like the one on page 44 and work through the five areas of design (set, lighting, sound, costume and props) for their production of the tale.
- Each group presents their ideas to the class. Discuss together the design concepts that are emerging.
- Change the groups around and try a different tale. It should contrast with the first tale chosen.
- **Reflective Log**: Students record what went well when working in groups thinking about design. What did they find challenging?

Give Extra Support: to groups who find it hard to make a decision about which tales to work on and to those who find coming up with an original design concept challenging. Help them to identify what the basic elements of mythical stories are, including key archetypes such as good vs evil, or virtues being rewarded and vices punished.

Challenge: those who work fast and complete the two tables in less than the given time. Ask them to research and draw aspects of the design.

CHECKING PROGRESS	Ask students to check their progress against the progress criteria on page 45 of the Student's Book and monitor their responses, making note of whether they have reached **Sound** or **Excellent** progress.

Unit 3.2   Exploring sets and stages – a learning sequence

SPOTLIGHT ON:	How can I use different stage and set options?

This learning sequence is designed to accompany the activities in Unit 3.2 of the Student's Book, with a focus on the demands of the practical examination. Teachers will be able to dip into and out of the activities, depending on the specific learning needs of the student group. Each section has been given an approximate time frame and, where a lesson is an average of an hour in length, we anticipate that the sequence might take up to three hours or three lessons.

KEY TERMS:
downstage, rake, stage layout/configuration, upstage

Learning outcomes:
- **Identify** the varying stage layouts and configurations that can be used for theatrical performances.
- **Explore** the different ways sound, lighting, props and costume can communicate the meaning of a piece of theatre in a given stage layout or configuration.

Differentiated learning outcomes:
- **All** students must explore the possibilities of a different stage layout and design for a play.
- **Most** students should be able to suggest ways to use set, lighting, sound, costume and props in a variety of stage configurations.
- **Some** students will be able to produce a sophisticated design concept for a short piece of theatre in a variety of stage layouts.

Resources:
- Student's Book: pp. 46–51
- Reflective Log
- Stage space
- Flipchart or computer/projector
- Coloured pens
- Old magazines and large sheet of paper suitable for making collages
- Handout 14: Mind map template
- (**Option**: Handout 23: Different types of stage space)

Syllabus Assessment Objectives:

AO1: Understanding repertoire
Candidates will be assessed on their ability to demonstrate knowledge and understanding of the possibilities of repertoire, and how to interpret and realise it in a live performance.

AO3: Acting skills
Candidates will be assessed on their acting skills and their ability to communicate effectively to an audience.

STARTING POINT (20 min)

Equipment: Internet access, flipchart or whiteboard, pens

- **Focus (10 min):** Ask the students to consider some of the performances they have seen and the type of venues they have visited. Encourage them to talk about the type of stage layouts that were used and where the audience were placed. As a class, on the whiteboard or flipchart, make notes on the advantages and disadvantages of each stage layout.

- **Option:** If possible, look through a variety of websites for different theatres and the stage layouts they use. You might be able to get access to the technical specifications of different theatres. Try the National Theatre in London and explore the different theatre spaces within it. Try smaller theatres such as Riverhouse on www.riverhousebarn.co.uk. This is a very small theatre seating an audience of 60 people, but nevertheless a variety of layouts can be used, including cabaret style. Reflect on how you might use the performance area.

- **Warm-up (10 min)**: Ask the students to walk to the 15 areas of the stage to familiarise themselves with the terminology. Ask them to find a space and lie down on the horizontal plane, then stand in the vertical plane, now in a trio, make the letter N with their bodies. The person in the middle, on the slant, is on what is called the sagittal plane. Explain how these three planes can be used when designing sets. Ask them to think about levels – high, medium and low – and how these might be used in designing an interior, for example a living room with furniture, or a king's court with a throne.

EXPLORING THE SKILLS (50 min)

Equipment: Student's Book, Reflective Log, a stage area, flipchart or whiteboard, pens, internet access, (Option – Handout 23)

- Ask students to look at the diagram showing the areas of the 'end on' stage on page 46 of the Student's Book. Explain the areas of the stage and the shorthand that can be used when writing about them – for example, DSL for downstage left, USR for upstage left, CS for centre stage.

- Ask the students to stand on the stage or in the performance space you have. Call out one area at a time e.g. CS (centre stage), and ask them to move there in a huddle. Do this for all of the areas until they feel happy with the terminology. Remind them that the areas are always from the actor's point of view (i.e. looking from the stage out to the audience).

- Students should then work in pairs to create journeys for each other, using the 15 areas of the stage in the 'end on' diagram. For example, student A asks student B to start USL (upstage left) and walk to DSC (downstage centre) then run to CSR (centre stage right) then to (RC) right centre. The journeys can be longer but must have a starting point, a destination and at least three moves in between. If you are working in a studio or classroom, this can be set up as an end on layout by putting in the first row of seats in the audience so that the actors know where the front of the stage is.

- Ask students to refer to pages 47 and 48 of the Student's Book and consider the other types of stage layout shown: proscenium arch, thrust, traverse, in-the-round and promenade. They should consider how each stage layout affects the vocal expression and physicality of the actors, the set design, costume, lighting and sound, as well as the sight lines for the audience. For each configuration, ask them, in groups, to discuss the advantages and disadvantages of the layout from the point of view of:
  - the actors
  - the director
  - the designers
  - the audience.

- Alternatively, you can hold a plenary feedback session, and summarise the points on the flipchart or whiteboard. **Note**: Students will discuss this topic again in Unit 4.5, and Handout 23 ('Different types of stage space') will be useful at that point. **Option**: You could distribute Handout 23 here in Unit 3, if you prefer.

- **Option**: Ask students to find examples on the internet of productions in theatres they know of around the world, using the different layouts. They should try to find images taken from productions in those venues that show detailed sets. They could then create a display using these images along with descriptive captions and brief information about the play.

- **Reflective Log**: Students should think about different configurations and staging, and note down what appeals to them and why. Ask them to think about what personal challenges they themselves might face as a performer in each of the configurations and which they would find more challenging.

DEVELOPING THE SKILLS (30–50 min)

Equipment: Student's Book, DVD player or computer with data projector and speakers

- Using page 49 of the Student's Book, discuss what is meant by the following terms: 'theatrical realism' and 'abstract set'.

- Ask the students to work through Questions 6 and 7 in small groups and then share opinions as a class. Discuss the details of the two sets, shown in the photographs, and how they help communicate the meaning and the style of the play.

- **Option**: Divide the stage into different areas to create 'rooms', mentally. Agree together what each 'room' might be (e.g. a bedroom, a court room, a classroom, a throne room, a garden shed, a small shop). The students should imagine each room is going to be a set for a play. Put a group of students in each 'room' and ask them to make a list of objects/furniture needed to create a modern-day, realistic setting in that room. Each group of students then gives feedback to the class about the objects/furniture they have listed in their particular room, and what purpose specific objects/furniture might have, in a play set in that room. Encourage them to contribute to the discussion about each other's rooms.

- **Option**: Show some DVD/clips from a variety of theatrical productions in order to discuss the types of set that are used – both realistic and abstract – and how effective students feel they are. To help you find appropriate plays, a list is given in the Examiner's Report each year, which centres have used for repertoire. The National Theatre in London has an archive of recordings of all plays that have been produced there as well as a bookshop with many DVDs of past productions (and an online ordering facility). Programmes of productions can also be useful if they have helpful photographs showing the set.

APPLYING THE SKILLS (90 min)

Equipment: Student's Book, Handout 14, Reflective Log, large sheet of paper, marker pens, internet access

- Ask students to work in groups to read quickly through the extract on pages 50–51 of the Student's Book. Consider the stage directions and ask the students to try to work out when the play is set and where the scene is taking place. They should notice that the actors have to break the fourth wall in this play (that is, they speak directly to the audience).
- Ask the students to perform the piece in different stage layouts starting with end-on and then trying in-the-round, traverse and promenade. Assess each layout and discuss the possibilities and challenges in staging the piece in each of the layouts.
- Ask the students to sketch a realistic set design for the piece. They will have to carry out research into the historical era and the geographical setting of the piece. Consider giving them some basic facts about the composers Mozart and Salieri and show some images of where Mozart lived and worked. More able students will be able to plan and conduct their own research.
- Look at costumes for men from the era. When considering costume design, look at fabric, cut, size, shape and colour. The neckline, length of sleeves, trousers and skirts are all very important, as these are often key signs of historical era. Think about the time of day in the extract and how the stage should be lit. Are there any key props needed?
- **Option**: Ask students to devise a short piece in small groups. The theme should be quite abstract – for example, 'Time'. This should be discussed and a mind map or spider diagram drawn up (use the template in Handout 14 if appropriate). Here are some ideas to think about:
  - phrases and sayings with the word 'time' – for example, 'Time waits for no man. Time is of the essence. Time and time again. This is the last time. I have no time. Where has the time gone? Time flies. There's no time like the present.'
  - images associated with time – for example, clocks, watches, ticking, the White Rabbit from *Alice in Wonderland* who says 'I'm late. I'm late.'
- Ask students to start by making frozen tableaux to illustrate some of the phrases or images above. The piece should be non-narrative. The students should make at least four tableaux and use transitions to link them. You might consider filming the piece, which will be an improvisation at this stage.
- Ask the students to suggest and, if possible, sketch ideas for a set, costumes, props, lighting and sound. These designs should be abstract rather than realistic.
- **Reflective Log**: Sketch designs for the *Amadeus* extract and the devised piece based on 'Time'.

Give Extra Support: to students who don't feel confident about their design and drawing skills. Using old magazines, show them how to use collage and mood boards to create design ideas.

Challenge: students with a talent for visual design by giving them different plays to design.

CHECKING PROGRESS	Ask students to check their progress against the progress criteria on page 51 of the Student's Book and monitor their responses, making note of whether they have reached **Sound** or **Excellent** progress.

Unit 3.3 Exploring lighting – a learning sequence

SPOTLIGHT ON:	How can I use light to enhance my practical work?

This learning sequence is designed to accompany the activities in Unit 3.3 of the Student's Book, with a focus on the demands of the practical examination. Teachers will be able to dip into and out of the activities, depending on the specific learning needs of the student group. Each section has been given an approximate time frame and, where a lesson is an average of an hour in length, we anticipate that the sequence might take up to three hours or three lessons.

KEY TERMS:
fresnel, gobo, par can, profile, rigging

Learning outcomes:
- **Identify** and **use** basic technical terminology for theatre lighting.
- **Explore** the importance of direction, intensity and colour in lighting design.

Differentiated learning outcomes:
- **All** students must be able to use basic technical terminology for theatre lighting and explore the possibilities of different lighting set-ups for a play.
- **Most** students should be able to suggest ways to use a variety of aspects of lighting to create mood and temporal setting (day/night, interior/exterior).
- **Some** students will be able to produce a sophisticated lighting design concept that can be used in a symbolic way.

Resources:
- Student's Book: pp. 52–55
- Handout 15: Lighting design table
- Flipchart or computer/projector
- Coloured pens
- Reflective Log
- Stage space with lighting rig

Syllabus Assessment Objectives:

AO1: Understanding repertoire

Candidates will be assessed on their ability to demonstrate knowledge and understanding of the possibilities of repertoire, and how to interpret and realise it in a live performance.

AO3: Acting skills

Candidates will be assessed on their acting skills and their ability to communicate effectively to an audience.

STARTING POINT (20–40 min)

Equipment: Student's Book, access to theatre, torches, flipchart or whiteboard, pens, Reflective Log

> **Focus (20 min)**: If you have access to a theatre, ask the students to sit in the auditorium and ask the technician to talk them through the different types of lighting effects and lanterns that can be used to create mood and atmosphere as well as different locations and times of day. For each effect ask a couple of students to stand on stage so the class can see how the lighting affects the look (angles and features) of the actors' faces and how feelings can be evoked, such as a red light for anger or passion. Ask the students how each lighting change makes them feel or what time of day they think it suggests.

> **Warm-up (20 min)**: Working with the technician, ask the students to stand on stage in various lighting states. They should begin by walking around the space and, on the teacher's instruction, stop and greet the nearest actor. Run this several times, at different times of day with appropriate greetings, such as the following:

- 'Good morning. Did you sleep well?'
- 'Good morning. Lovely day, isn't it?'
- 'Good afternoon, looks like rain...'
- 'Good evening, what a chilly night!'
- 'Such a clear night. Look at the stars!'
- 'Wow, have you seen the full moon?'

➢ For each greeting the technician should change the lighting to an appropriate state. Once this has been rehearsed, split the students into two groups and run it again for each group so that students can watch and appreciate the difference the lighting can make. You could start by running the sequence in natural light or house lights, then again with the lighting changes.

➢ If you do not have access to a theatre, then show some images from the Student's Book and/or from theatre websites to stimulate discussion. Use torches to create different lighting effects on stage and experiment with direction to see how it can alter mood.

➢ **Reflective Log**: Give the students the following list of words and phrases and write them in a table format on a whiteboard: back projection, battens, blackout, colour filter, colour mixing, cross fade, downlight, flood, focus, gel, gobo, ground rows, house lights, lantern, profile lantern, rigging, specials. Ask the students to find definitions for each one and record them in their Reflective Log. (Definitions can be found online and most of these terms are included in the Cambridge IGCSE Drama specification, which can be downloaded at: www.cie.org.uk/programmes-and-qualifications/cambridge-igcse-drama-0411.)

EXPLORING THE SKILLS (40 min)

Equipment: Student's Book, rigged lighting and a stage, computer and data projector

➢ Look at the table on page 53 in the Student's Book, which shows the different types of lantern: par can, fresnel and profile. If you have access to a theatre with rigged lighting, show the students the effects that each type of lantern can create and ask them to suggest ideas about when it might be used in a play. They might like to use their own devised work as the focus of the discussion.

➢ Consider how to light a set showing an interior such as a living room. Ask students questions about lighting such as: Where would the lighting sources come from and how would you show this? Consider where the windows are and how to show daylight coming through. If there is a spotlight above a prisoner on a chair in a cell, how does this increase the idea of an interrogation?

➢ Ask students to consider the impact of using colours to create warm or cold 'temperatures' in an exterior setting such as a beach on a very sunny day (by using orange and reds), or a snow-covered mountain on a cold day (using blue and white). Ask students to reflect on the impact of different effects, such as using a wash or lighting small areas of the stage with a profile lantern where the shutters can control the spill of light. If possible, illustrate these ideas with appropriate lighting in the theatre.

DEVELOPING THE SKILLS (30 min)

Equipment: Student's Book

➢ Discuss three aspects of lighting with the class: direction, intensity and colour.

- Direction: Experiment with creating shadows on stage and perhaps lighting from the floor upwards. Use a screen and create silhouettes or a puppet show just using your hands. Students should be able to stand on stage and feel the light on their faces when using spotlights. Explain that you can also follow an actor with a follow spot. Try using torches if necessary. Discuss the potential impact of a selection of gobos to create different settings such as a forest.
- Intensity: This refers to the brightness of the lantern and is on a spectrum from low to high. You can increase the intensity to show time passing by making it look as if the sun is getting hotter towards midday and then lessening the intensity to make it seem that the day is moving towards evening.
- Colour: Refer students to page 54 of the Student's Book and ask them to do Questions 3, 4 and 5. ➢ Students share their ideas as a whole class.

APPLYING THE SKILLS (45 min)

Equipment: Student's Book, Handout 15, Reflective Log, rigged lighting

- Ask the students to read the extract from *A Streetcar Named Desire* by Tennessee Williams on page 54 of the Student's Book, and then to work in pairs or individually through Questions 7–10 on pages 54–55. Ask students to annotate the speech as suggested in Questions 8 and 9 and to include this in their Reflective Log. Use the table in Question 9 to record their decisions (or use Handout 15).

- Students should choose either a group repertoire piece or a group-devised piece and draw a lighting plan for each scene. Before they do this, they will need to think about and discuss the performance style of the piece and decide whether it has a realistic or abstract set. Encourage students to look at each scene in detail and pay careful attention to the stage directions. They should make notes on the following:
    - mood and atmosphere
    - temporal setting – when it is happening (time of day, season, historical period)
    - spatial setting – where it is happening (interior/exterior; type of weather; type of building (whether a private home or office, or a public space such as a church)
    - effects that might need to be created – for example, prison bars, disco lights or lights coming from a glitter ball in a ballroom, light and shade in a forest, or the effects of water such as rain.

- If you do not have access to a lighting rig, do not worry. As long as the actors can be seen, that is the main point of performance. In their written work, students might be asked about lighting design, so they would find it useful to make some notes about how lighting is used in productions they have been to see at the theatre or have watched on DVD (ideally a recording of a live performance in the theatre). The website www.digitaltheatre.com is a useful resource for watching recordings of live theatre.

- **Reflective Log**: Students should include copies of annotated speeches and scripts for repertoire and devised pieces illustrating their ideas about use of lighting and lighting effects.

> **Give Extra Support:** to students who find it difficult to visualise a design or who are colour-blind by discussing the range of possibilities of angles, using photographs of productions.
>
> **Challenge:** students who are vocal in discussion and have lots of lighting ideas (but no way of fulfilling their designs in practical terms) to research a range of theatre venues and lighting designers.

CHECKING PROGRESS	Ask students to check their progress against the progress criteria on page 55 of the Student's Book and monitor their responses, making note of whether they have reached **Sound** or **Excellent** progress.

Unit 3.4 — Exploring sound – a learning sequence

| **SPOTLIGHT ON:** | How can I use sound to enhance my performance pieces? |

This learning sequence is designed to accompany the activities in Unit 3.4 of the Student's Book, with a focus on the demands of the practical examination. Teachers will be able to dip into and out of the activities, depending on the specific learning needs of the student group. Each section has been given an approximate time frame and, where a lesson is an average of an hour in length, we anticipate that the sequence might take up to three hours or three lessons.

KEY TERMS:
sound design, sound effects

Learning outcomes:
- **Explore** the different ways sound can create a setting.
- **Identify** different sound effects that can be used and how they can add to a performance.

Differentiated learning outcomes:
- **All** students must explore the possibilities of creating and using different sound settings for a play.
- **Most** students should be able to suggest ways of using sound to enhance character and further action.
- **Some** students will be able to recognise a signature sound for a character, use sound to make transitions smooth and introduce appropriate sound effects in a production.

Resources:
- Student's Book: pp. 56–57
- Handout 16: Sound design table
- Reflective Log
- Flipchart or computer/projector
- Coloured pens
- Some instruments such as keyboard, guitar, percussion
- Computer, tablet, data projector

Syllabus Assessment Objectives:

AO1: Understanding repertoire
Candidates will be assessed on their ability to demonstrate knowledge and understanding of the possibilities of repertoire, and how to interpret and realise it in a live performance.

AO2: Devising
Candidates will be assessed on their ability to devise dramatic material and reflect on its effectiveness.

STARTING POINT (30 min)

Equipment: Sound system, DVD or laptop with data projector

- **Focus (20 min):** *Pirates of the Caribbean.* Play the opening sequence of a famous film that has a strong music score, such as the first *Pirates of the Caribbean* film. The first 2–3 minutes should suffice. Play the sequence again without the music and ask the students to comment on the difference in atmosphere, character and plot. Play the soundtrack only on the third playing of the sequence. Can the students spot where moments in the sequence are enhanced by the music?

- Use the focus task to lead into a short discussion about the function of sound in a performance.

- **Warm-up (10 min):** Begin with a 'Stomp'-style sequence (**Note:** if the students are unfamiliar with this contemporary rhythm and dance performance, you can look at examples from the Stomp show, online. There are several examples on YouTube). Use various everyday objects, such as brooms, a pair of spoons, chopsticks, a large metal bin, saucepans, and buckets or washing-up bowls. Make sure that every student has an object to 'play' as if it were a musical instrument. You can set this up in whatever way works best for the objects that the students will be playing, but an example might look like this: the brooms begin with one rhythm, perhaps two slow beats followed by two fast beats. The spoons join in with four fast beats then a rest. The saucepans add a variation of the beat, followed by the washing-up bowls. Each object has its own rhythm which sits around the main underpinning rhythm. In turn, all the objects join in and build up the piece, using the brooms as the underpinning rhythm. After practising for several minutes until the students understand how the collaboration of the various 'instruments' works, discuss together how movement from the players (the students) could be introduced alongside the piece. Run this again with movement, using as much of the stage space as possible.

EXPLORING THE SKILLS (30 min)

Equipment: Student's Book, Reflective Log, film sound tracks, recorded sound effects, speakers for computer or CD player

- Experiment with sound effects that actors can make themselves on stage, such as when slapping someone across the face. Ask how this can be achieved without injury. One actor mimes slapping another's face; the person who has been slapped turns their head away as a reaction and the actor doing the slapping, slaps their own leg to make the sound. (The slapped leg must be upstage so not seen by the audience, or the effect will be ruined.)

- Ask the students to think about other sounds that might arise from a fight or an argument, such as breaking glass or breaking furniture. For these, recorded sound effects can be found on the internet or on pre-recorded compact discs. They can be amplified by the sound-mixing desk operated by the theatre technician, or by students who are interested in the technical side of theatre. You could illustrate the variety of sound effects available by playing a number of them from the internet or CD.

- Next play three pieces of music and ask the students to discuss how the different pieces make them feel. Choose film scores from a thriller film, a romantic film and a comedy. Ask the students to listen carefully to discern which instruments are being played and why. You could ask musical students how major and minor keys are used to change the mood and emotions. How are some film scores used to denote historical and geographical settings?

- Students can then work on Questions 2 and 3 on page 56 in the Student's Book, in pairs or small groups.

- **Reflective Log**: Ask students to note down their reflections on the impact of specific sound effects.

DEVELOPING THE SKILLS (60 min)

Equipment: Student's Book, Handout 16, Reflective Log

- Students should work through Questions 4 and 5 on page 57 of the Student's Book, in pairs or small groups. It might be helpful to have them step outside the classroom or performance area and stand silently listening intently for every sound they can hear, in order to attune their listening skills for the smallest of sounds as well as the louder sounds around them.

- Discuss the different types of sound with students – functional (a sound linked to the context and used to convey something about the progression of the story or plot), atmospheric (a sound that generates an emotional reaction from the audience) and incidental (a sound that has no particular importance of purpose, but adds to the general interest), and ask them to complete Handout 16 (the different categories of sound design).

- Students should consider the following places and imagine the types of sounds they might hear in these places. Then working in small groups, the students should try to create a soundscape to conjure up at least two of the following settings for the audience:
  - a busy garage
  - a railway station
  - the beach in summer
  - a busy restaurant
  - a shopping mall
  - a hairdressing salon.

- **Option**: Students can put the scenes in an order of their choice and link them with a loose plot idea – for example, a character has lost their purse/wallet or an important letter and retraces their steps to find it, visiting some of these places. They should create the incidental music that plays between each scene and signifies the characters travelling from one place to another.

- **Reflective Log**: Ask students to summarise their ideas in their Reflective Log.

APPLYING THE SKILLS (45–50 min)

Equipment: Student's Book, Reflective Log, computer, recording equipment (either professional or simply a smart phone)

- In pairs or small groups, students work on Question 6 on page 57 in the Student's Book, then share their ideas with the whole class.
- Students should consider their own work, both repertoire and devised, group and individual. Discuss in the group how sound might be used in each to enhance mood, reflect character, create smooth transitions and evoke emotions. It might help speed up or slow down the pace of an acting sequence.
- Students should now experiment with their ideas. Recorded sound effects should be put on a CD or in a file so that the sound technician can use this during the performance of their piece. The effects should be numbered and cued by number in the annotated script so that the technician knows when to play them. The CD or file must be given to the technician in time for the technical rehearsal when they can use the tracks and see if they work with the performance. Sound is as important as lighting and needs to be given time to develop to make a strong piece of theatre. Sound effects that are not correctly synchronised can be comical!
- **Reflective Log**: Students should make notes on soundscapes and effects, and annotate scripts for performance pieces as appropriate.

Give Extra Support: to students who do not respond instinctively to music, by using language to describe pictures created by sound – for example, battle scenes for loud, classical music.

Challenge: those who play instruments or enjoy mixing tracks to compose a short piece of music for their devised piece.

CHECKING PROGRESS	Ask students to check their progress against the progress criteria on page 57 of the Student's Book and monitor their responses, making note of whether they have reached **Sound** or **Excellent** progress.

Unit 3.5 Using props – a learning sequence

SPOTLIGHT ON:	How can props help me in my practical work?

This learning sequence is designed to accompany the activities in Unit 3.5 of the Student's Book, with a focus on the demands of the practical examination. Teachers will be able to dip into and out of the activities, depending on the specific learning needs of the student group. Each section has been given an approximate time frame and, where a lesson is an average of an hour in length, we anticipate that the sequence might take up to three hours or three lessons.

Learning outcomes:

- **Explore** the different ways props can be used to enhance character, further plot and complement setting.

Differentiated learning outcomes:

- **All** students must be able to suggest a variety of different props for a play and outline their use and function.
- **Most** students should be able to suggest ways to use props to enhance character and further action.
- **Some** students will be able to design their own props that are appropriate to function and setting.

Resources:

- Student's Book: pp. 58–59
- Reflective Log
- A selection of props, such as a walking stick, handbag, suitcase, mobile phone, pad of paper and pen
- Flipchart or whiteboard and marker pens
- Copies of extracts from three scripts (see 'Applying the skills')

Syllabus Assessment Objectives:

AO1: Understanding repertoire

Candidates will be assessed on their ability to demonstrate knowledge and understanding of the possibilities of repertoire, and how to interpret and realise it in a live performance.

AO3: Acting skills

Candidates will be assessed on their acting skills and their ability to communicate effectively to an audience.

STARTING POINT (20 min)

Equipment: selection of images of people at work, lightweight ball

- **Focus & Warm up**: Ask the students to stand on stage in a circle. Using a lightweight plastic football, throw the ball at one student after saying their name. After catching the ball, the student chooses another person, shouts their name and throws the ball at them. Use a smaller ball if the area is small. Warn students not to throw the ball too high.

- Speed the game up by throwing the ball faster. Someone might drop the ball, which is what you want to happen so it may have to be the teacher who drops the ball. You are trying to demonstrate the fact that an actor must rehearse with his props to avoid making mistakes like dropping them or not knowing where they are on stage.

- Show some images of people at work and ask the class to state what is the main prop for each one. For example, the key signifying prop for the job of postman/woman is their bag with letters in it.

EXPLORING THE SKILLS (30 min)

Equipment: Student's Book, flipcharts or whiteboard, coloured pens, tray of miscellaneous props

- Ask the students to imagine some famous characters from fiction such as Sherlock Holmes, Alice in Wonderland, Huckleberry Finn, Little Red Riding Hood, the Snow Queen, the White Rabbit, Spiderman, Batman and Oliver Twist (adapt the list of 'famous' characters to suit the cultural background of your students). Next ask them to think of a prop associated with each character. Discuss whether the character would be able to function without the prop.

- On the flipcharts or whiteboard give the students a list of jobs, such as butcher, baker, plumber, doctor and nurse. For each one choose a prop that can signify their job – for example, a stethoscope for a doctor. Discuss whether the audience would recognise the character's profession if they did not have the prop. Ask students if the character should always have the prop with him. What does a prop tell an audience, that a costume does not?

- Refer students to page 58 of the Student's Book and discuss what is meant by personal props. Consider props such as glasses, pens, letters and bags and what they might communicate about the character.

- Prepare a table of props for the students to look at and handle. They should choose a prop and become the character they associate with that prop. Ask them to work in small groups to improvise around the idea of speed dating or a birthday dinner. This should be a short improvisation lasting 5–10 minutes. The aim is that each character finds out as much as they can about the other characters in their group.

DEVELOPING THE SKILLS (60 min)

Equipment: Student's Book, flipchart or whiteboard, pens

- Ask the students to read the short extract from the play *The Madness of George III,* on page 59 of the Student's Book. You may need to explain a little bit about the play and the king's illness. (Some people said that the king was suffering from a rare disease called porphyria, which may have caused his mental disturbances and made his urine turn blue. His medical records show that he was given a medicine based on gentian, which is a plant with deep blue flowers, so this could be the reason for the blue urine.)

- Ask the students why the chamber pot has to be made of glass in this scene and whether the prop is embellishing the character and/or furthering the plot (Questions 2 and 3 on page 59).

- Students should then discuss Question 4. Tell students that if this is the first discovery of the king's blue urine, it could be a very important moment in the play, and therefore music has been used to underscore this discovery (marking the moment).

- Ask the students to think about their own work in both repertoire and devised contexts and go through their scripts, picking out clues for the use of props. They should make a list of props for each piece. As a developmental task they could do this for their monologues as well.

- Explain that some scripts have detailed stage directions, while others have very few, so the clues for use of props are in the dialogue. Some practitioners prefer to use mime instead of introducing props into a production. The stage manager must make sure that all props are in the correct places, both on and off stage, at the beginning of each performance. Actors must practise with props and become used to them. They should use them in rehearsals. It is a mistake to introduce props in a dress rehearsal or first performance, as this may lead to errors during the performance. Discuss this with the students, asking them to come up with some examples of things that could go wrong if actors haven't practised enough with the props.

- As a whole group, think about what props they might need for scenes set in the following locations, (some of these formed the focus of activities in Unit 3.4):
  - a busy garage
  - a railway station
  - the beach in summer
  - a busy restaurant
  - a restaurant
  - a hairdressing salon.

- Help students to draw up a table by modelling the format on the whiteboard/flipchart. List the locations below in the first column. In the second column, they should write the characters they would expect to meet there and in the third column, they should list the props they would expect the characters to have in each location. In the fourth column, they should write other props they would expect to see in the location. The table should look something like the one shown on the next page.

Location	Characters in that location	Props the characters might have	Other props in the location
A busy garage			

APPLYING THE SKILLS (45 min)

Equipment: Student's Book, computer with data projector, selection of extracts from play scripts

- Students answer Question 5 on page 59 of the Student's Book then share feedback with the class.

- **Option**: Choose various script extracts from different plays, representing three different historical periods and forms. Ask students to work in groups, each with one script extract. The students decide on who plays which part and then they read through the extract. They look for clues in the stage directions and the dialogue to see what props are needed and make a list of them, stating whether they are personal or hand props to be brought onstage. Each group works through each of the extracts, recording the props list for each.

- Ask students to imagine an abstract set. Ask them to discuss whether they would still expect to see props in this style of drama. If so, what might these props be and what might they be like? You could look at clips or images on the internet from plays such as *The Curious Incident of the Dog in the Night-Time* (by Simon Stephens, based on a novel by Mark Haddon), or *His Dark Materials* (adapted for the stage by Nicholas Wright and based on the books by Phillip Pullman).

Give Extra Support: to students who miss details when reading stage directions by helping them to focus on specific parts of the script or particular stage directions.

Challenge: students who are good at making things or resourcing items. Give them a list of props for their devised or repertoire pieces and ask them either to identify the materials required to make a specified prop or to suggest ways of sourcing each prop.

CHECKING PROGRESS	Ask students to check their progress against the progress criteria on page 59 of the Student's Book and monitor their responses, making note of whether they have reached **Sound** or **Excellent** progress.

Unit 3.6 — Using costume and make-up – a learning sequence

SPOTLIGHT ON:	How can I use costume to embellish my characterisation?

This learning sequence is designed to accompany the activities in Unit 3.6 of the Student's Book, with a focus on the demands of the practical examination. Teachers will be able to dip into and out of the activities, depending on the specific learning needs of the student group. Each section has been given an approximate time frame and, where a lesson is an average of an hour in length, we anticipate that the sequence might take up to three hours or three lessons.

Learning outcomes:
- **Identify** the different ways costume can be used to enhance character and complement setting.
- **Explore** the reasons for using stage make-up and different approaches to make-up design.

Differentiated learning outcomes:
- **All** students must explore the different possible options for costume and make-up for a play and outline their use and function.
- **Most** students should be able to suggest ways to use costumes/make-up to enhance character and further action.
- **Some** students will be able to design/source their own costumes/make-up that are appropriate to function and setting.

Resources:
- Student's Book: pp. 60–63
- Reflective Log
- Handout 17: Make-up design template
- Permission sheets for students (school template)
- Some examples of costumes, either the real costume or images/clips
- Make-up boxes with foundation, powder, eye liners, eye shadows, lipsticks, brushes, sponges
- Rail of costumes and accessories for a range of characters and periods
- Wigs and masks

Syllabus Assessment Objectives:

AO1: Understanding repertoire
Candidates will be assessed on their ability to demonstrate knowledge and understanding of the possibilities of repertoire, and how to interpret and realise it in a live performance.

AO3: Acting skills
Candidates will be assessed on their acting skills and their ability to communicate effectively to an audience.

STARTING POINT (50 min)

Equipment: Student's Book, DVD player or computer and projector and speakers, rail of costumes and accessories for a range of characters and periods

- **Focus (30 min)**: Show some appropriate film clips from period dramas on television or film where the costumes display different features to reflect the changing fashions of the time in the country in which the film is set. Show images of fashion in various centuries and decades, for example 1920s, 1960s, 1980s and now. Ask students to comment on the changes in the style of shoes, the cut of dresses and trousers, the length of shirt collars, the width of ties, the height of men's trousers and the length of skirts.

- Ask students to consider what costume can tell you about character, such as the character's status or social class, age and personality. Use some images from plays or films, from across a range of genres and historical eras to inspire the discussion.

- Then ask the students to discuss Questions 1 and 2 on page 60 of the Student's Book.

- Ask students to consider the make-up designs in shows such as *Cats, Animal Farm, Lord of the Flies* and *Hamlet*. Show images from different shows, including Japanese and Chinese productions, and comment on the use of make-up. Is it natural-looking or exaggerated, melodramatic, or even pantomime-like?

- Ask students to find their own images of costume and make-up for stage and bring the images to class to share.

- **Warm-up (20 min)**: Prepare the stage with a selection of costumes. These could be placed on a rail and/or around the space on chairs and tables. Guiding the students, ask them to choose a costume and try it on. The costumes chosen should be loose fitting, for example coats and jackets, perhaps some dresses, skirts and tops that could be put on over rehearsal clothes. Remember to include accessories such as hats, wigs, shoes and bags to accompany the main costume. Each student should have a costume to wear.

  Now ask them to become the character of the costume and hold a conversation with another student about their mutual friend who has a problem at work. While the conversation happens, the two characters should be walking through a garden. Ask the students to discuss how the costume led them to the character and how they felt when walking in the costume. Could they envisage any problems with wearing costumes in general?

EXPLORING THE SKILLS (25 min)

Equipment: Student's Book, flipcharts or whiteboard, coloured pens, images of characters from stage productions, DVD player or computer and projector with speakers

- **Costume**: The job of a costume designer involves collaboration with the director, the producer and other designers as well as the other actors. The following website explains the job in detail:
http://artsalive.ca/collections/costumes/designer_role.php?lang=en

- **1. Working with the director, producer and design team**

  Explain the relationship between the costume designer and the director. If you are designing or choosing a costume, you need to know what the overall aesthetic of the production is so that the costume will be complementary. You do not want colours to clash with the set unless this is a conscious decision on the part of the set designer. If the play is written by an earlier playwright such as Shakespeare, you need to know in what period the director has chosen to set the play; for example, it could be during the Second World War, in the early 1940s. You would then need to study this era and look at costumes, accessories and make-up that could be appropriate for the characters in the production. You need to discuss the directorial concept for the play with the director so that you are in keeping with this concept in your designs. If you want a historically accurate portrayal of character in a period drama, then do not use fabrics or colours that were not available in that historical period.

- **2. Working with the cast**

  Explain the relationship between actors in the ensemble and the costume designer. When working with the actor, you will need to see that the costume is appropriate in terms of wearabilty (is it comfortable?), durability (will it last?) and flexibility (can you move in it?). Actors will have to attend sessions where they are measured so that the costume can be made to fit them and any adjustments identified that are needed for a perfect fit.

- **3. Working with the lighting team**

  Explain the relationship between actors, director, lighting designer and costume designer. It is important to check what every costume looks like under stage lights as it will reflect whatever light is present. For example, a white costume representing innocence can be changed to red with lighting in order to signify lust, passion, anger or danger.

- **4. Working with the sound team**

  Explain the relationship between actors, director, sound designer and costume designer. Beware of the sounds a costume can make when the actor moves and find out if microphones will pick up these sounds and relay them to the audience, as this could undermine the quality of the performance.

  Option: Have a look at the scenes in the film *Singin' in the Rain*, which is about the advent of talking movies, where Lena plays with her pearls and the microphone picks up all the crunching sounds! Use search terms on YouTube: 'Singin' in the Rain (6/8) Movie clip – Out of Synch (1952)'.

- Ask students to work through Questions 3 and 4 on pages 60–61 of the Student's Book. Note students' ideas on a flipchart or whiteboard.

DEVELOPING THE SKILLS (60 min)

Equipment: Student's Book, Handout 17, brushes, sponges, eye shadows, foundation/panstick, mascara, eye-liners, lipsticks, paper tissues, cotton wool, make-up remover or face wipes, bowl of water

- **Stage make-up**: Explain to students that stage make-up is a complex art and requires a specific skill set. Make-up artists often train extensively for the job and the course fees can be very high. There are degree courses and these usually require students to have an art portfolio. It is not only about being artistic in using products but also about having knowledge about the skin and eyes. This is why courses are often long and expensive, as there is a science behind the beauty of the make-up and prosthetics. The best way to understand stage make-up is to have an expert come and do a workshop, but if this is not possible, then students can practise on each other using stage make-up.

- Look at the images of different types of make-up on page 62 and discuss which styles of theatre are being portrayed and what can be deduced about the characters. Students should sketch ideas for different make-up designs using Handout 17 if appropriate.

- **Option**: if possible set up a classroom with mirrors and make-up stations where the artist/you as demonstrator has access to brushes, sponges and various types of make-up as in a beauty salon.

  - Before applying any make-up, the make-up artist must always have the written permission of the model and a signed declaration that they have no allergies to make-up or cosmetic products. (The teacher should complete a basic risk assessment and have a contingency plan in case a student has a reaction to any of the products used. Consult with the school nurse as appropriate and follow agreed school protocols.)

  - Start with the idea of face painting and use images of animal faces for the first set of made-up faces. Some students could try minimal, more natural looking make-up and others could try different characters from different ages and social classes.

  - Once made up, the models/actors should go onstage under the lights to see what the make-up looks like. The artists should take photographs of their models and discuss the effects of the make-up in their pairs.

APPLYING THE SKILLS (45 min)

Equipment: Student's Book, Reflective Log, computer with internet access, programmes of past productions with images of characters in costume, selection of masks, wigs, rail of costumes

- Ask students to read page 63 of the Student's Book and work on Questions 6–8 with a partner.

- Students should consider the characters they are playing in their repertoire monologues and design a costume for the character. They should consider all aspects, including shoes, bags, hats, scarves and other accessories, and should make sure the design is in colour. If it is for a period piece, they must research the fashion of the time. For a group piece of repertoire, they need to make sure the costumes work alongside each other. Ask them to research past productions of the two different plays and look at images of the costumes.

- The students should now consider the type of make-up for the character, the style of the piece, the historical period and the size of the theatre space. You could tell them that ballet dancers wear very heavy stage make up such as three lines for the eyes and a red dot on the point of the eye nearest the nose, pinkish blusher, red lipstick and foundation. This is because they have to project to a very large auditorium.

- **Option**: Students should work through the various performance spaces as described in Unit 3.2 and discuss what type of make-up might be appropriate for each one. Fantasy pieces are the most exciting to design.

- The students could investigate how prosthetics are used in the theatre and take notes.

- The following video is useful for showing more about stage make-up:
www.nationaltheatre.org.uk/video/costume-wigs-and-make-up-at-the-national-theatre

- Introduce hairstyling, wigs and masks as other aspects of costume. Some cultures use masks in their theatre more than others. When using masks, it is worth considering how the vocals will sound if the mouth is covered; half masks are easier to work with in this respect. Students should experiment with masks to see how they might want to use them in a production. Masks can look fantastic, but they can also be a real challenge to work with as they are often heavy, they can restrict actors' vision, and they can make actors feel hot, uncomfortable and even claustrophobic.

➢ **Reflective Log**: Students should create clearly labelled sketches for costume and make-up designs and reflect on what aspect of costume and make-up design they find most interesting and stimulating. Which aspect do they find most challenging and difficult? How could they improve their creativity in this area?

Give Extra Support: to students who struggle with research into costume design. For example, if a student has to design or source a costume for a period drama, show them books which illustrate costumes for different historical periods and occupations.

Challenge: students who are good at making things or resourcing items. Give them a list of costumes for their devised or repertoire pieces to make or source.

| CHECKING PROGRESS | Ask students to check their progress against the progress criteria on page 63 of the Student's Book and monitor their responses, making note of whether they have reached **Sound** or **Excellent** progress. |

Unit 3.7   Applying the skills – a learning sequence

SPOTLIGHT ON:	How can I bring all design elements together?

This learning sequence is designed to accompany the activities in Unit 3.7 of the Student's Book, with a focus on the demands of the practical examination. Teachers will be able to dip into and out of the activities, depending on the specific learning needs of the student group. Each section has been given an approximate time frame and, where a lesson is an average of an hour in length, we anticipate that the sequence might take up to three hours or three lessons.

Learning outcomes:
- **Identify** the different aspects of design for an extract.
- **Explore** the different ways sound, lighting, props and costume can communicate the meaning of a piece of theatre.

Differentiated learning outcomes:
- **All** students must explore the role of a designer for a play.
- **Most** students should be able to suggest ways to use set, lighting, sound, costume and props in a given scene.
- **Some** students will be able to produce a sophisticated design concept for a short piece of theatre, bringing together set, costume, lighting and sound in a cohesive manner with a clear aesthetic.

Resources:
- Student's Book: pp. 64–67
- Reflective Log
- Flipchart or computer/ projector
- Internet access
- Coloured marker pens / pencils
- A3 paper

Syllabus Assessment Objectives:

AO1: Understanding repertoire

Candidates will be assessed on their ability to demonstrate knowledge and understanding of the possibilities of repertoire, and how to interpret and realise it in a live performance.

AO3: Acting skills

Candidates will be assessed on their acting skills and their ability to communicate effectively to an audience.

STARTING POINT (20 min)

Equipment: Student's Book

- **Focus (10 min)**: Recap as a whole class the elements of design covered in Units 3.1 to 3.6 and discuss why they must work together in a production.

- **Warm-up (10 min)**: Ask the students to walk around the space, weaving in and out of each other as if they are at a crowded market place. It is hot and the time is 12 noon. Every so often, they should stop and barter with a market trader or look at an object on a market stall. They feel hungry and thirsty and stop at a café for an early lunch or a snack and a drink. It is Saturday and the market closes in 15 minutes.

  Give them this information while they are walking so that they can take in the details. You might place the market in a particular country (depending on where your school is) – make it a country they could be familiar with but not the one they are living in.

  After the exercise, bring them back to a circle and hold a plenary, asking questions concerning how they would create the scene using set, lighting, props, costume and sound.

EXPLORING THE SKILLS (30 min)

Equipment: Student's Book

- Ask the students to work in groups of four and read through the speech on pages 64–65 of the Student's Book from *Trojan Women* by Greek playwright Euripides (c. 488–406 BCE). Note that you might need to explain what this date means. One of the students should read Hecuba and the other three the Chorus. Discuss Question 1 on page 65.

DEVELOPING THE SKILLS (50 min)

Equipment: Student's Book, Reflective Log, computer and internet access

- Ask students to investigate productions of the play *Trojan Women*, focusing on the four main design elements (set, lighting, costume and sound). Students should keep notes on which productions they look at by stating the date of the premiere and where it took place, as well as the names of the director / producer / designers of set, lighting, costume and sound. If they find images, they should print them off and stick them in a notebook, labelling them with the name of the character and the actor playing the role.

- **Option**: Ask students to annotate any images they have collected with comments relating to:
  - type of configuration (in-the-round, proscenium, thrust etc.)
  - historical era
  - colour, texture and shape of costumes
  - any details about hairstyle, wigs, masks and make-up
  - personal and hand props
  - type of set (realist, abstract, fantasy, expressionist, minimalist)
  - lighting design
  - details about sound design.

- Students should read through pages 65–66 of the Student's Book, working on Questions 2, 3 and 4, based on *Trojan Women*. In pairs or trios, students should answer the questions and fulfil the tasks – some might be set for homework.

- Once the students have worked through all the aspects of design for *Trojan Women*, they should start work on their own repertoire monologues. They should follow the same structure as above by researching past productions. The notes and designs should be placed in their Reflective Log. Some theatres show interviews with designers talking about their work, which could be useful as part of the research process.

- **Reflective Log**: Students should research into past productions of their repertoire pieces, and consider any design elements they might want to include in their own performances.

APPLYING THE SKILLS (2 × 45 min)

Equipment: Student's Book, Reflective Log, A3 paper and pens, pencils

- Students now need to apply the same process of researching and designing for a production.

- Students should return to the ideas they had for their devised pieces and use the process they employed when coming up with designs for *Trojan Women* and their monologues. This time, working in small groups, they should decide and allocate design roles as well as the role of director. The director must take the lead in creating the design concept, while the designers must come up with designs in keeping with this concept. They should work together to create the designs for set, props, lighting, costume, make-up and sound, sketching their ideas on the paper provided.

- As a second stage, ask the students to follow the same process for the group repertoire piece, as appropriate.

- Read the sample student answers on page 67 of the Student's Book, outlining ideas for design for *Trojan Women*. Ask students to try Questions 5 and 6.

- **Reflective Log**: Ask students to write about their own design concepts for the group-devised piece, making sure that they address all the design elements.

- **Reflective Log**: Students should add their designs to their Reflective Log or draw them straight in, and comment on the reasons behind their design decisions.

Give Extra Support: to students who find it hard to come up with a design concept for their piece of repertoire or devised work. Give them ideas about specific productions to research.

Challenge: those who work quickly and finish their designs early. Ask them to change their design concept for a given production or elements of the design to increase the sense of juxtaposition (the placing of two opposites next to each other to heighten the contrast, such as good vs evil, black vs white, master and servant, contrasts in wigs, masks, pancake, colours and texture).

CHECKING PROGRESS	Ask students to check their progress against the progress criteria on page 67 of the Student's Book and monitor their responses, making note of whether they have reached **Sound** or **Excellent** progress.

Unit 4.1 Responding to stimuli – a learning sequence

| SPOTLIGHT ON: | How can I come up with interesting dramatic ideas from a given stimulus? |

This learning sequence is designed to accompany the activities in Unit 4.1 of the Student's Book, with a focus on the demands of the practical examination. Teachers will be able to dip into and out of the activities, depending on the specific learning needs of the student group. Each section has been given an approximate time frame and, where a lesson is an average of an hour in length, we anticipate that the sequence might take up to three hours or three lessons.

KEY TERMS:
evolve, impressionistic

Learning outcomes:
- **Identify** the possibilities of different devising stimuli.
- **Explore** different approaches to devising for an audience.

Differentiated learning outcomes:
- **All** students must take part in devising activities and explore a range of different approaches to working with other actors in a devising context.
- **Most** students should shape and alter the way a devised piece is performed to communicate meaning to an audience.
- **Some** students could devise original solutions to dramatic problems to create impact for an audience.

Resources:
- Student's Book: pp. 70–73
- Reflective Log
- Handout 14: Mind map template
- Computer/projector with internet access
- Flipchart or A1 paper and pens
- Coloured pens

Syllabus Assessment Objectives:

AO2: Devising
Candidates will be assessed on their ability to devise dramatic material and reflect on its effectiveness.

AO3: Acting skills
Candidates will be assessed on their acting skills and their ability to communicate effectively to an audience.

Written work
Candidates' written answers should show practical and theoretical understanding of the play extract and devised piece they have performed as part of the course. They may need to write about a variety of aspects of:
- acting (e.g. interaction, pacing, physicality, proxemics, role, vocal expression)
- devising (e.g. characterisation, contrast, structure, tension)
- directing (e.g. advice to actors, directorial concept, mood, staging)
- design (costume and make-up, lighting, props, scenography, set, sound).

STARTING POINT (30–50 min)

Equipment: Student's Book, Handout 14

➤ **Focus (10 min)**: Working as a whole class, ask students to identify a range of dramatic stimuli that might be used as starting points for devising and create a group mind map (use Handout 14 to help if appropriate).

➤ **Warm-up (20 min)**: 'Chinese whispers'. This activity is designed to develop group awareness, by introducing the students to the idea of an evolving story and giving them an example of the development of a story that starts in a simple format. The students form a circle and the teacher introduces a short sentence in whispered format to one person in the circle and they then pass it on exactly as they heard it to the next person in the circle. The sentence is then passed around the circle until it arrives back at the start and can be spoken out loud again. The difference in format and content can be quite startling! An example of a suitable sentence is as follows: 'The small brown dog became very muddy and had to be bathed by its irritated owner.'

- In pairs or small groups, students discuss Questions 1 and 2 on page 70 of the Student's Book. Encourage the students to think beyond what looks obvious in the photograph – for example, has the young man been rejected by his peer group for some reason? What could the reason be? Discuss the range of possible characters. Students should feed back their ideas to the whole class.

EXPLORING THE SKILLS (30–60 min)

Equipment: Student's Book, Reflective Log, computer/projector, internet access

- Introduce the concept of impressionism by showing the picture of Gustave Caillebotte's most famous and ambitious impressionistic painting *Paris Street, Rainy Day*, exhibited at the Third Impressionist Exhibition in Paris in 1877, where it was not well received by the critics. (Images of this painting are readily available on the internet.) Despite its poor initial reception, this picture is considered by many contemporary art historians to be one of the best representations of 19th-century Paris ever painted. Ask students, working in pairs, to discuss the range of possible stories that might emerge from the 'impression' made by the painting.

- Return to the photo on page 70 of the Student's Book and discuss the three possible stories offered in the table, as outlined in Questions 3 and 4 on page 71. Discuss the particular challenges facing actors in staging any of these stories.

- Divide the students into groups of three to six people, allocating to each group one of the three options to use as a basis for a short improvised scene (Question 5 on page 71). Give students an opportunity to stage the scenes for comment by an audience of their peers.

- **Reflective Log**: Give students five minutes to write up observations, as instructed on page 71. What did I do and why did I do it? What are the challenges involved in devising from a photo?

DEVELOPING THE SKILLS (30 min)

Equipment: Student's Book, Reflective Log, Handout 14, flipchart or whiteboard, pens

- Discuss with the students how ideas can evolve, through discussion. Look together at the conversation in the tinted panel on page 71 of the Student's Book. Explain that various approaches can be taken to a stimulus to enable the ideas to evolve, including:
  - generating a mind map (spider diagram), as in Handout 14
  - running a short improvisation
  - running a group discussion.

- Discuss the elements of a dramatic story (an opening, a problem, a climax, a resolution). You might like to draw a flow chart on a flipchart or whiteboard and explore each element in turn. Look at the spider diagram / mind map on page 72.

- As a group, read the poem 'First Frost' printed on page 72 of the Student's Book. Through discussion, identify the main character, scene and situation (Question 10, page 73). Create a hot seat for the character by asking one of the students to take on the role. Explore:
  - who or what has hurt the girl
  - what has happened to her prior to her appearance in the phone box
  - what might happen next.

- **Reflective Log**: Give students five minutes to copy the flow chart or spider diagram, and create some notes on the character, using the questions above.

APPLYING THE SKILLS (30–60 min)

Equipment: Student's Book, Reflective Log, simple props for devised scenes

- As a group create a 'soundscape' for the day of the phone call, suggesting ideas for the scenes before the girl's appearance in the phone booth. Examples could be: the sounds of a party, snatched conversations, sound of heels on a floor, running, car doors, phone dialling tone. With students sitting in a circle, ask each person to add a sound to the sound created by the first contributor, gradually building a chorus or soundscape.

- Ask students to move into small groups and begin to identify a possible series of key moments for the story. Ask students to form a series of tableaux to bring key images to life – remind them of the importance of levels and clarity for an audience. Ask students to add some of the sounds from the soundscape to the transitions between the images – this will create a short dramatic sequence. As a challenge they could also try to add some dramatic dialogue.
- **Option**: Introduce students to the 'split-screen' device, where the stage is split into two halves (a split screen). Ask two students to take the stage on the left half, and two students to take the stage on the right half. The players on the stage right half begin a scene while the other half remains frozen. Where there is a word or phrase that the players on the stage left half could use as a beginning to their scene, they repeat it and begin the scene from that point. When this happens, the stage right players freeze. The two halves continue their scenes, each freezing when the other is performing. Students can explore different scenes involving the girl in the phone booth, for example an argument with parents or a scene at work.
- **Option**: In small groups students should now begin to devise a short piece based on the key images and ideas that they have come up with. They can use the table on page 73 for help if appropriate.
- **Reflective Log**: Give students five minutes to record their observations, including key dramatic terms and the key images and characters they have come up with.

Give Extra Support: by working with an identified group of students or sets of pairs who might struggle and create a mind map with them. Once they have seen some possibilities, they can go away and begin to use improvisational techniques to create the world of the character.

Challenge: more able students by encouraging them to create a short script for the 'First Frost' story.

CHECKING PROGRESS	Ask students to check their progress against the progress criteria on page 73 of the Student's Book and monitor their responses, making note of whether they have reached **Sound** or **Excellent** progress.

Unit 4.2 — Structuring devised work – a learning sequence

SPOTLIGHT ON:	How can I contribute effectively to devised work in terms of its organisation and structure?

This learning sequence is designed to accompany the activities in Unit 4.2 of the Student's Book, with a focus on the demands of the practical examination. Teachers will be able to dip into and out of the activities, depending on the specific learning needs of the student group. Each section has been given an approximate time frame and, where a lesson is an average of an hour in length, we anticipate that the sequence might take up to three hours or three lessons.

KEY TERMS:
contrast, genre, *commedia dell'arte*

Learning outcomes:
- **Identify** the possibilities of using different devising stimuli to create original drama.
- **Explore** different approaches to crafting and structuring devised pieces.

Differentiated learning outcomes:
- **All** students must take part in devising activities and explore a range of different approaches to working with other actors in a devising context.
- **Most** students should shape and alter the way a devised piece is performed to communicate meaning to an audience.
- **Some** students could devise original solutions to dramatic problems to create impact for an audience.

Resources:
- Student's Book: pp. 74–77
- Reflective Log
- Handout 14: Mind map template
- Handout 18: Plotting a typical *Commedia* storyline
- Flipchart or large sheet of paper and pens
- Coloured pens

Syllabus Assessment Objectives:

AO2: Devising

Candidates will be assessed on their ability to devise dramatic material and reflect on its effectiveness.

AO3: Acting skills

Candidates will be assessed on their acting skills and their ability to communicate effectively to an audience.

Written work

Candidates' written answers should show practical and theoretical understanding of the play extract and devised piece they have performed as part of the course. They may need to write about a variety of aspects of:

- acting (e.g. interaction, pacing, physicality, proxemics, role, vocal expression)
- devising (e.g. characterisation, contrast, structure, tension)
- directing (e.g. advice to actors, directorial concept, mood, staging)
- design (costume and make-up, lighting, props, scenography, set, sound).

STARTING POINT (40 min)

Equipment: Flipchart or white board and pens, Handout 14

> **Focus (10 min)**: As a whole class group, ask students to identify the range of possible stimuli for a devised piece and create a group mind map; they should try to group the stimuli into visual, aural and kinaesthetic stimuli (use Handout 14 to help if appropriate).

- **Warm-up (10–20 min):** 'Once upon a time'. The group sit in a circle and the teacher takes on the role of the chief storyteller. The storyteller begins the story with the line 'Once upon a time...' and hands the story to the next person who picks upon on the previous detail: for example, 'Once upon a time there was a beautiful princess...' – Person 2: 'who sat looking thoughtfully across her mountain range'. The group should be encouraged to respond spontaneously and not to hesitate. The story can continue to circle until it has reached its natural conclusion. Emphasise the mythical basis of stories that often contain moral messages and archetypes.

- As a whole class, discuss with students the narrative graph on page 74 of the Student's Book – explain the key elements of the narrative: exposition, rising action, climax, falling action, resolution.

- Review the poem 'First Frost' on page 72 of the Student's Book, and discuss where within the narrative structure the girl first receives the phone call (Questions 1 and 2). Using one of the hypothetical stories discussed in Unit 4.1, students work together to draw the graph and plot the exposition, climax and resolution.

EXPLORING THE SKILLS (30–60 min)

Equipment: Student's Book, Reflective Log

- Read the example for the T. S. Eliot poem on page 75 ('The Hollow Men'), and discuss the concept of contrast (see the 'Key terms' definition near the bottom of that page). Ask students to create an 'essence machine', using the words 'hollow' and 'men'. One student moves into the centre of a circle with a movement and a sound (which could be a word or syllable), which they repeat. Others join one at a time, latching on to a part of the body of the previous person, and create a group machine that expresses the 'essence' of the phrase 'hollow men'. Discuss the contrasts in shape, sound and texture that might be useful in creating a piece of drama here.

- In groups students should work through Questions 3 and 4, developing and expanding the 'hollow men' ideas, by thinking about different scenes, new characters, possible dialogue and how to add contrast. Encourage them to keep to the narrative arc (exposition, rising action, climax, falling action, resolution).

- **Reflective Log:** Give students five minutes to write up their observations from this work on narrative, and on how to include contrast. They should ask: What did they do and why did they do it? What are the challenges involved in devising from a photographic stimulus?

DEVELOPING THE SKILLS (30 min)

Equipment: Student's Book, Handout 18, computers with internet access

- Discuss the concept of 'genre' in relation to the example of *Commedia dell'arte* given on page 76 of the Student's Book.

- **Option:** Ask students to research the genre of *Commedia dell'arte* and to identify other characters that typically appear in this genre.

- Ask students, working in pairs, to complete the table given on page 76 (also reproduced as Handout 18).

- To answer Question 6, groups should compare their ideas and agree the best storyline. Students then prepare a short improvisation to perform for the class.

- Discuss and explore with them the key timeline terms introduced on pages 76–77: flashback, flash-forward, parallel scenes and rewind.

- Ask students to work in small groups to create a narrative graph for 'The Hollow Men', on page 75, which includes identification of dramatic characters. Ask them to devise a short sequence of images that tell the story through flashback – they will therefore start at the climax point of the narrative and work backwards. They should start with the image and subsequently add words and sounds. They can then speed up or slow down the sequence, as they develop it.

APPLYING THE SKILLS (30–60 min)

Equipment: Student's Book, Reflective Log, simple props for devised scenes

- As a group, read the headline on page 77 of the Student's Book. Discuss the possible range of characters, narrative arc and appropriate genres.

- **Option:** Set up two chairs to act as a doctor's waiting room. The teacher acting in role plays the part of the doctor, calling through each of a series of characters, who enter the surgery to tell their stories. Students can work in role as the patients, nurses, parents and friends. The improvisation should focus on the development of character, motivation and dramatic tension. Develop the drama by adding a flashback or flash-forward sequence. Focus on the specific actions created and identify any gestures that might be associated with an emerging character.

- **Option**: In small groups, students should start to devise a short improvised sequence that tells the story set out in the article from *The Independent*. You might want to replace the article with an alternative relevant to the time and context of the group.
- **Reflective Log**: Give students five minutes to record their observations including key dramatic terms and the key images and characters which they have come up with.

Give Extra Support: by working with an identified group of students or sets of pairs who might struggle and create a mind map with them. Once they have seen some possibilities, they can go away and begin to use improvisational techniques to create the world of the character.

Challenge: encourage more confident students to create a short script for the 'First Frost' story.

CHECKING PROGRESS	Ask students to check their progress against the progress criteria on page 77 of the Student's Book and monitor their responses, making note of whether they have reached **Sound** or **Excellent** progress.

Unit 4.3 — Effective group work – a learning sequence

| SPOTLIGHT ON: | How can I make sure I contribute positively to group work? |

This learning sequence is designed to accompany the activities in Unit 4.3 of the Student's Book, with a focus on the demands of the practical examination. Teachers will be able to dip into and out of the activities, depending on the specific learning needs of the student group. Each section has been given an approximate time frame and, where a lesson is an average of an hour in length, we anticipate that the sequence might take up to three hours or three lessons.

Learning outcomes:
- **Identify** the skills required to work effectively as a group in devising for performance.
- **Explore** different approaches to devising for an audience.

Differentiated learning outcomes:
- **All** students must take part in evaluating their own developing skillset.
- **Most** students should consider their contribution to the different stages of devising for an audience.
- **Some** students could devise original solutions to a thematic stimulus to create impact for an audience.

Resources:
- Student's Book: pp. 78–79
- Reflective Log
- Handout 19: Stages of devised work
- Handout 20: Group roles
- Flipchart or large sheet of paper and pens
- Coloured pens
- Reflective Log

Syllabus Assessment Objectives:

AO2: Devising

Candidates will be assessed on their ability to devise dramatic material and reflect on its effectiveness.

AO3: Acting skills

Candidates will be assessed on their acting skills and their ability to communicate effectively to an audience.

Written work

Candidates' written answers should show practical and theoretical understanding of the play extract and devised piece they have performed as part of the course. They may need to write about a variety of aspects of:
- acting (e.g. interaction, pacing, physicality, proxemics, role, vocal expression)
- devising (e.g. characterisation, contrast, structure, tension)
- directing (e.g. advice to actors, directorial concept, mood, staging)
- design (costume and make-up, lighting, props, scenography, set, sound).

STARTING POINT (30 min)

Equipment: Reflective Log

> **Focus (10 min):** Ask students, as a whole class group, to draw up a short comparative two column table in their Reflective Log listing what they think are their strengths and areas for development in group-work skills – for example, 'confident in working with my peers', 'full of creative ideas', 'need to listen better to others'.

> **Warm-up (10–20 min):** 'Lost'. This warm-up activity will help students to develop an imaginative sense of being lost and alone. Ask students to lie on the ground, or relax sitting on chairs with their eyes closed. Ask them to imagine that they find themselves lost in a particular landscape or space. Talk them through the moment that they find themselves alone and ask them to imagine the physical response to this situation by placing focus in every part of the body from feet to scalp.

➢ Ask them to look around the imaginative space and then begin to explore marking their awareness of how they feel to be alone and lost in this landscape or space. Bring students back to full consciousness slowly and up to sitting/standing on the count of 10.

EXPLORING THE SKILLS (30–60 min)

Equipment: Student's Book, Reflective Log, Handout 19

➢ As a whole class, ask students to discuss the table on page 78 of the Student's Book. Using Handout 19 ('Stages of devised work'), encourage students to add a personal comment in the third column of the table, such as 'I always come up with good ideas quickly when devising, but feel others don't listen so I need to be more assertive about putting my ideas forward.' Students can give themselves marks out of 5. After they complete the table they should then stick it into their Reflective Logs.

➢ **Reflective Log**: Students consider the challenges they face when working in a group and what they could change to improve the experience.

DEVELOPING THE SKILLS (30 min)

Equipment: Student's Book, Reflective Log, Handout 20

➢ Working through Questions 3 and 4, encourage students to share with their peers what they feel their strengths are, and where there are areas for improvement and development. **Option**: Use Handout 20 to help inform the discussion if appropriate. Discuss with the students the range of roles that might be useful in an effective group situation. If appropriate, give out the role cards from Handout 20 when groups come together for group work. Remember to swap the role cards around so that individual students have a different role at different times.

➢ **Reflective Log**: Give students five minutes to create some notes on the preferred roles within their group. For greater challenge, ask them to reflect on and subsequently explain the reason for their own role preference.

APPLYING THE SKILLS (30–60 min)

Equipment: Student's Book, Reflective Log, flipchart or whiteboard, pens

➢ As a whole class, brainstorm possible stories emanating from the theme 'Lost and alone' (Question 5, page 79 of the Student's Book). Write up ideas on the flipchart or whiteboard, in the form of a mind map or spider diagram.

➢ Ask students to create a series of tableaux illustrating the theme. They should identify key characters in the story and begin to highlight physical characteristics that could be developed and/or exaggerated. Refer to *commedia* characters as appropriate – refer back to Unit 4.2 as appropriate.

➢ **Reflective Log**: Give students five minutes to record observations on the various stages of the devising of a sequence in response to the theme – use prompts if helpful: What did I do? Why was it helpful?

Give Extra Support: by working with an identified group of students or sets of pairs who might struggle and create a mind map with them. Once they have seen some possibilities, they can go away and begin to use improvisational techniques to create the drama.

Challenge: by encouraging students to create a short script for the 'Lost and alone' story.

CHECKING PROGRESS	Ask students to check their progress against the progress criteria on page 79 of the Student's Book and monitor their responses, making note of whether they have reached **Sound** or **Excellent** progress.

Unit 4.4 Communicating meaning – a learning sequence

SPOTLIGHT ON:	How can I communicate effectively to an audience during devised work?

This learning sequence is designed to accompany the activities in Unit 4.4 of the Student's Book, with a focus on the demands of the practical examination. Teachers will be able to dip into and out of the activities, depending on the specific learning needs of the student group. Each section has been given an approximate time frame and, where a lesson is an average of an hour in length, we anticipate that the sequence might take up to three hours or three lessons.

KEY TERMS:
insight, monologue, ritual

Learning outcomes:
- **Identify** the skills required to shape a role in a devised performance.
- **Explore** how the role can link to the overall devised concept.

Differentiated learning outcomes:
- **All** students must take part in developing a role.
- **Most** students should develop the physical and vocal attributes of a dramatic role.
- **Some** students could devise a range of roles in a dramatic narrative to create impact for an audience.

Resources:
- Student's Book: pp. 80–83
- Photographs
- Handout 21: Character back story table
- Handout 22: Role on the wall
- Flipchart or A1 paper and marker pens
- Reflective Log

Syllabus Assessment Objectives:

AO2: Devising
Candidates will be assessed on their ability to devise dramatic material and reflect on its effectiveness.

AO3: Acting skills
Candidates will be assessed on their acting skills and their ability to communicate effectively to an audience.

Written work
Candidates' written answers should show practical and theoretical understanding of the play extract and devised piece they have performed as part of the course. They may need to write about a variety of aspects of:
- acting (e.g. interaction, pacing, physicality, proxemics, role, vocal expression)
- devising (e.g. characterisation, contrast, structure, tension)
- directing (e.g. advice to actors, directorial concept, mood, staging)
- design (costume and make-up, lighting, props, scenography, set, sound).

STARTING POINT (20–30 min)
Equipment: Student's Book, Handout 22

> **Focus (10–15 min):** Ask students, in pairs, to complete a 'role on the wall' (Handout 22) for a character that they created from either their work on 'First Frost' in Unit 4.1 or 'Lost and Alone' in Unit 4.3. Explain to students that they should add the thoughts and feelings of the character to the inside of the figure, while on the outside of the figure they write down what others might say about the character.

> **Warm-up (10–20 min):** 'Leading Body Parts'. This activity will help students to develop a sense of physical awareness. Students walk around the room, led by the teacher, who encourages them to adopt a neutral posture, developing awareness of the focus of energy in their everyday walk. The group will begin to develop an awareness of the energy in the room and the teacher can change the pace and

quality of movement by issuing instructions and introducing commands such as 'stop', 'start',' turn', 'clap', 'jump' and so on.

Students are then asked to notice the focus of energy in the body and begin to allow that body part to lead their movement. Pace can then be increased or decreased.

EXPLORING THE SKILLS (30–60 min)
Equipment: Student's Book, Reflective Log, images of people who have survived extreme weather conditions

- Ask students, as a whole class, to consider the picture on page 80 of the Student's Book. Ask them to physically respond to the photographic image, using the structure, 'Begin... Then... Finally...', as set out on page 80. Discuss the centre of energy in the developing character (the place in the body where there is greatest energy and which generates the movement).

- As a whole class group, read the newspaper headline 'Left high and dry, but refusing to leave'. Discuss the possible context that might have generated this headline. If appropriate, show some photographic images from flooded areas. Repeat the physical unfolding exercise as a character hidden during a terrible event, who emerges from their hiding place. Work through Questions 2 and 3 on page 80.

- **Option**: Consider the examples of scenario development set out in the table on page 81 of the Student's Book. For Question 4, students should choose one of the examples and begin to create a series of movements and gestures in order to shape a sequence.

- Read the student interpretation of the flood victim set out on page 81 (in the tinted panel). Discuss the focus on specific details and the use of contrasts in movement and gesture in the paragraph.

- **Reflective Log**: Ask students to write a paragraph on the creation of the role, using the following questions as prompts: What did I do? How did I do it? What did I learn?

DEVELOPING THE SKILLS (30–60 min)
Equipment: Student's Book, Reflective Log, Handout 21

- As a whole class, read the role profiles set out in the pink grid on page 82 of the Student's Book. Discuss the connection between the role profile and the overall 'devised concepts' suggested. You may need to explain the nature of a 'devised concept' by referring to themes such as the impact of global warming and the link to human attributes such as greed, courage and so on. Discuss the dramatic potential of the various concepts or scenarios by considering the potential emotional impact on an audience and contemporary relevance.

- For Questions 5 and 6 on pages 82 and 83, ask students to choose one of the characters from the grid and then work on their own to complete a 'back story table' for that character (they can use Handout 21 for this purpose). They should then work with a partner to share the details. Suggest that they could use hot-seating questioning to develop the role further, if they wish.

- **Option**: Ask the pairs to then develop a 'park bench' improvisation where the characters meet for the first time, introducing themselves and exchanging stories. A more confident pair can then perform the improvisation for the rest of the group. Develop this exercise by evaluating the quality of movement, gesture and facial expression. Remind them to consider their 'centre of energy' and leading body part.

- The group now needs to be reminded of the relationship between the specific individual characters being created and the overall concept that they might be working with. For Question 8, ask students to consider the photo on page 83 of the Student's Book and discuss as many aspects of the scene as they can:
    - What proxemics can be seen in the picture? What different levels are there?
    - How does use of proxemics and levels fit into the overall concept?
    - What do the characters' gestures and movements imply?
    - What about the different characters' costume?
    - What possible interpretation of specific characters might an audience make?
    - How is lighting used in this scene and how does it serve the overall concept?

- **Reflective Log**: Record possible ideas for a devised concept in relation to the stimulus.

APPLYING THE SKILLS (30–60 min)

Equipment: Student's Book, Reflective Log, camera (video or still)

➢ Move pairs into larger groups and ask them to develop a short devised piece using either the headline or photo on page 80 of the Student's Book. Remind them to consider using some of the dramatic strategies already introduced, including a soundscape, split screen, movement sequences using different pace and quality, music, and character monologues. The piece should last 5–10 minutes and include a couple of developed characters. You could consider taking some photos of the group work to use in the evaluation session in Unit 4.5.

➢ **Reflective Log**: Give students five minutes to record observations on the various stages of the devising of a sequence in response to the theme.

Give Extra Support: by working with an identified group of students, or sets of pairs who might struggle, and develop the hot-seating exercise with them by offering prompt questions about the character's work, job or family. Once the students have seen some possibilities, they can try using improvisational techniques to develop the roles.

Challenge: more confident students to write a short monologue for their flood character in their Reflective Log.

CHECKING PROGRESS	Ask students to check their progress against the progress criteria on page 83 of the Student's Book and monitor their responses, making note of whether they have reached **Sound** or **Excellent** progress.

Unit 4.5 — Evaluating and responding – a learning sequence

SPOTLIGHT ON:	What makes an effective self-evaluation?

This learning sequence is designed to accompany the activities in Unit 4.5 of the Student's Book, with a focus on the demands of the practical examination. Teachers will be able to dip into and out of the activities, depending on the specific learning needs of the student group. Each section has been given an approximate time frame and, where a lesson is an average of an hour in length, we anticipate that the sequence might take up to three hours or three lessons.

KEY TERMS:
promenade performance, self-evaluation

Learning outcomes:
- **Identify** the skills required to write effectively about their own devised work.
- **Understand** how the development of an individual role can link to the overall concept.

Differentiated learning outcomes:
- **All** students must take part in self-evaluation activities.
- **Most** students should be able to describe, analyse and evaluate their own work.
- **Some** students could reflect on the relationship between their own work and that of others.

Resources:
- Student's Book: pp. 84–87
- (Option: Handout 23: Different types of stage space)
- (Option: Handout 24: Drawing ground plans)
- Flipchart or large sheet of paper and pens
- Coloured pens and highlighters
- Reflective Log
- Copies of text from page 84 of the Student's Book

Syllabus Assessment Objectives:

AO2: Devising

Candidates will be assessed on their ability to devise dramatic material and reflect on its effectiveness.

AO3: Acting skills

Candidates will be assessed on their acting skills and their ability to communicate effectively to an audience.

Written work

Candidates' written answers should show practical and theoretical understanding of the play extract and devised piece they have performed as part of the course. They may need to write about a variety of aspects of:
- acting (e.g. interaction, pacing, physicality, proxemics, role, vocal expression)
- devising (e.g. characterisation, contrast, structure, tension)
- directing (e.g. advice to actors, directorial concept, mood, staging)
- design (costume and make-up, lighting, props, scenography, set, sound).

STARTING POINT (30–40 min)

Equipment: Student's Book, copies of text from page 84 of the Student's Book, highlighter pens

> **Focus (10–20 min)**: To introduce the evaluative conceptual framework of strengths and areas for development, ask students to read the student response on page 84 of the Student's Book. Ask them, working on their own, to identify the areas that they consider have been effective and then areas that they have identified as needing to be developed further (Questions 1 and 2). Use this activity to remind students of the balancing nature of evaluating strengths and areas for development.

- **Warm-up (10–20 min)**: 'Remember that day'. This activity is designed to develop physical memory and self-awareness in performers. The teacher thinks of an activity that they might use to begin the day and says, for example, 'After I woke up, I stretched'; the teacher then performs the action of stretching. The next student repeats the sentence, together with the movement, and adds something: 'After I woke up, I stretched (stretching); then I danced to the bathroom (dancing).' The warm-up finishes when everyone in the circle has added an action and there is a complete sequence. Encourage all participants to focus on the detail behind each action.

EXPLORING THE SKILLS (30–60 min)

Equipment: Student's Book, Reflective Log, (Option: Handout 23)

- Ask students, working as a whole class, to consider the extract from the longer response on page 85 of the Student's Book. Discuss the questions that follow (Question 4, page 85), and check students' understanding of the different options for staging. (**Option**: Use Handout 23, Different types of stage space, or revisit aspects of Chapter 3 for support as appropriate – Unit 3.2 in particular.)

- **Reflective Log**: Ask students to reflect back to the flood piece (developed in Unit 4.4) and write some brief notes on staging choices. Ask them to try to pinpoint any moments that might emerge from the narrative arc of the piece and whether it would be useful to change the staging space for these moments – try to develop a small sketch of the stage space and any key design features including levels.

DEVELOPING THE SKILLS (30–60 min)

Equipment: Student's Book, (Option: Handout 24)

- As a whole class, consider the sample student notes in the table on page 86, which aims to capture the evolution of the devising concept emerging from work on the village.

- Ask students to work on Questions 5–7 in groups and then feed back to the whole class.

- Direct students to the two sample student responses on page 87. After reading these over, students should work on Question 8, and practise writing a paragraph or more describing the overall concept for their own devised work. They should then share what they have written with a partner, for feedback.

- **Option**: Students could consider again the staging choices set out in the third column of the table on page 86 of the Student's Book. If you would like to spend more time on this (30 minutes or more), and to offer greater challenge, put students into small groups and ask them to create a ground plan of proscenium-arch staging to reflect the decisions being made in Week 2. You could use Handout 24 to help here. You may wish to ask students to draw the template for a proscenium arch-staging onto a flipchart or a large piece of paper, then discuss the plans as a whole class.

- Ask students to read again the reflective paragraph written by Student B on page 87 of the Student's Book and discuss the decisions this student made in creating the role of the Chief.

APPLYING THE SKILLS (30–60 min)

Equipment: Student's Book, Reflective Log

- Ask students to read the two sample students responses on page 87 again and write some comments on how effectively the two sample responses show the development of character in the piece about the villagers and the well. Which of the points made in either of the two responses particularly stand out?

- **Option**: Ask students to begin to move around the room and consider the character of the village Chief who is facing the drought of the village and the greed of some of the villagers. Ask them to begin to locate the centre of energy for the character and allow that to affect their movement and posture. Ask them to think of an appropriate representative gesture for the character. They should imagine that they are walking towards some of their villagers and use the gesture to identify themselves and their status as Chief.

Ask the students to imagine they are walking up to the top of a hill outside of the village, where they will be able to look down at the well. Ask them to consider the physical impact of this view on the character. Consider taking some digital photos of students in role at this point and sharing them to evaluate the physical characterisation the students achieve.

Ask the students to come out of role and write a short monologue for the Chief that expresses their thoughts at this moment. Now ask students to work in pairs and nominate one of the pair to act as performer and the other as director. Give students five minutes to rehearse a short monologue for the Chief.

Encourage some of the students to perform and facilitate an evaluative discussion that focuses on the decisions being made by performers about movement, gesture, facial expression and posture for the Chief.

➢ **Reflective Log**: Give students five minutes to record observations on the decisions being made by the performers creating the role of the Chief. Use the various physical skills of movement, gesture, posture and facial expression as subheadings to help structure note-making here.

Give Extra Support: by working with students who find self-evaluation challenging to try to identify the decisions they have made as either performers or members of a group. Read the longer reflective passage on page 85 of the Student's Book and use highlighters to identify key phrases.

Challenge: students to write a response in relation to an extended question. See the Drama section of the Cambridge International Education website for access to these documents:

www.cie.org.uk/programmes-and-qualifications/cambridge-igcse-drama-0411/past-papers

CHECKING PROGRESS	Ask students to check their progress against the progress criteria on page 87 of the Student's Book and monitor their responses, making note of whether they have reached **Sound** or **Excellent** progress.

Unit 4.6 Applying the skills – a learning sequence

| SPOTLIGHT ON: | How can I plan, perform and evaluate my devised work to the best of my ability? |

This learning sequence is designed to accompany the activities in Unit 4.6 of the Student's Book, with a focus on the demands of the practical examination. Teachers will be able to dip into and out of the activities, depending on the specific learning needs of the student group. Each section has been given an approximate time frame and, where a lesson is an average of an hour in length, we anticipate that the sequence might take up to three hours or three lessons.

Learning outcomes:
- **Identify** the skills required to plan, prepare and perform a devised piece of work.
- **Explore** how the choice of stimulus can affect the devised outcome.

Differentiated learning outcomes:
- **All** students must take part in devising and evaluating their own work.
- **Most** students should be able to describe, analyse and evaluate their own work.
- **Some** students could reflect on the evolution of the devised concept in relation to the stimulus.

Resources:
- Student's Book: pp. 88–93
- Handout 25: Timeline flashcards
- Handout 14: Mind map template
- Flipchart or A1 paper, marker pens, and highlighters
- Reflective Log
- Music and CD player or computer with speakers
- Copies of the poem 'Demeter' from page 89 of the Student's Book

---

Syllabus Assessment Objectives:

AO2: Devising
Candidates will be assessed on their ability to devise dramatic material and reflect on its effectiveness.

AO3: Acting skills
Candidates will be assessed on their acting skills and their ability to communicate effectively to an audience.

Written work
Candidates' written answers should show practical and theoretical understanding of the play extract and devised piece they have performed as part of the course. They may need to write about a variety of aspects of:
- acting (e.g. interaction, pacing, physicality, proxemics, role, vocal expression)
- devising (e.g. characterisation, contrast, structure, tension)
- directing (e.g. advice to actors, directorial concept, mood, staging)
- design (costume and make-up, lighting, props, scenography, set, sound).

STARTING POINT (40 min)

Equipment: Student's Book, Reflective Log, copies of the poem 'Demeter' from page 89 of the Student's Book, Handout 14, Handout 25, A3 paper and pens

> **Focus (5 min)**: Ask students to work on their own to create a mind map for Stimulus 1, 'An unexpected arrival'. Use Handout 14 as appropriate. Ask them to record anything that comes to mind when they consider the stimulus. After three minutes ask students to share their ideas and images. Some could be encouraged to draw their ideas.

> **Warm-up (15–20 min)**: The following warm-up activities are designed to generate understanding of the key interpretative skills required to develop ideas in relation to images and words offered by stimulus materials.

- Choral storytelling: Seat the group in a circle and provide them with an opening line that will then form the basis of a group narrative – for example, 'There once was a small mouse who lived in a high tower.' Each contributor has to respond immediately to the line used by the previous storyteller. Allow the story to continue until everyone has contributed to it. This activity promotes group cohesion and develops confidence in the use of imagination.
- 'What am I doing?': Ask students to stand in a circle and ask for a volunteer, who is given a location and an action to improvise for the rest of the group. The volunteers is asked 'What are you doing?' and responds by describing their action – the action changes when another volunteer moves into the circle.

➢ **(15–20 min)**: Direct students to Questions 1 and 2 on pages 88–89 of the Student's Book. Give them 3–4 minutes to consider Stimulus 2, the painting *Le Pont de l'Europe*. Then they should share some initial responses. Ask the group for their first impressions of the use of colour, light and shade (especially shadow), and the actions of all of the visible characters.

➢ Divide students into small groups. Each group is given a set of timeline cards, BEFORE, DURING and AFTER (Handout 25). Ask each group to create one minute's worth of silent action that displays the activity of a different character in the painting along a timeline – for example, the man looking over the bridge may previously have had a violent disagreement with another man outside a café, then walked angrily along the bridge to get some fresh air and calm himself down. Each silent scene stops as the characters reach their frozen positions inside the picture frame. Groups should then discuss what happens to each character after the scene in the painting, and should develop a short piece of silent action to show that. Groups can then put the before and after pieces together to form a timeline for different characters in the painting.

➢ **Option**: Give students five minutes to read Stimulus 3, the poem 'Demeter', as a group. Divide students into different small groups. Ask students to create a series of three frozen tableaux highlighting the key images in the poem. For extra challenge students can create transitions using music and then adding captions.

➢ Direct students' attention to Questions 3 and 4, on page 89. Students should discuss the possible narratives that might emerge from the stimuli (e.g. around possible themes of anticipation and disappointment; travel and refuge; the cycles of the moon; abduction, mother/daughter relationships) and make a choice about which of the three stimuli to use for a piece of devised work. Encourage the students to create a mind map to brainstorm their ideas.

➢ **Reflective Log**: Give students five minutes to record the exercise using a simple grid answering questions such as: What did I do? Why did I do it? What did I learn?

EXPLORING THE SKILLS (30–40 min)
Equipment: Student's Book

➢ Impress upon students the importance of effective and thorough note-taking from the outset when planning devised work. Look together at a few different ways of doing this, outlined on page 90 of the Student's Book, and any other ways they might have ideas about.

DEVELOPING THE SKILLS (60 min)
Equipment: Student's Book, Reflective Log, sound system, music

➢ Students are now able to opt to explore one of the three stimuli further. Ask them to use the frozen tableaux or one-minute improvisation to develop an extended soundscape and movement sequence that would express a theme or idea that they would like to work with. **Option**: Use appropriate classical music to help stimulate ideas.

➢ After five minutes ask students to identify and discuss the key characters and storylines that they might take forward.

➢ Students should now be encouraged to create a group concept (e.g. mother–daughter relationships) and a short script for the devised piece. (As suggested in Question 6 on page 91, students can refer to examples of scripts in Chapters 2 and 6.)

➢ Students can begin to experiment with staging a couple of their key scenes. Remind them not to lose their developed images and sounds. You could use a metaphorical framework to help them move away from literal staging and dialogue – for example, 'a mother's grief is like the slow crumpling of a crisp bag'. After 15 or 20 minutes show a few of the scenes and evaluate the skills that are emerging and the staging decisions being made. Ask students to focus specifically on design aspects and how they might develop ideas for set and props.

- **Reflective Log**: Give students five minutes to record observations of the process including key dramatic terms. Ask them to reflect on what they did, why they did it and what impact their decisions had on the audience.

APPLYING THE SKILLS (30 min)
Equipment: Student's Book, Reflective Log

- Students can now be given a sample question to respond to and extend their evaluative skills. Use the exemplars on pages 91 and 92 of the Student's Book. Use the table on page 91, which offers a possible structure for an extended response. Give students 15 minutes to draft a short response to this question and share with a partner.

- As a whole group read the two sample student responses to Question 10a) (the analysis of the devising concept) on pages 92 and 93. Spend a few minutes on Question 12 on page 93, in particular working through the annotations that highlight the successes in the second response.

- Ask students to do Question 13, writing their own response to Question 10a). Encourage them to focus clearly on the link between the original stimulus and the concept they have developed.

Give Extra Support: by working with an identified group of students or sets of pairs who might struggle to script a devised piece of drama. Try to support the development of different kinds of dialogue and remind students to consider the use of pauses to build tension. Show them a page from a script to remind them of the layout of the script.

Challenge: students to combine ideas for design with their devised movement and language sequences. Offer selected props or musical instruments to help them.

CHECKING PROGRESS	Ask students to check their progress against the progress criteria on page 93 of the Student's Book and monitor their responses, making note of whether they have reached **Sound** or **Excellent** progress.

Unit 5.1 What is repertoire? – a learning sequence

SPOTLIGHT ON:	What is repertoire and how can I extend my knowledge of different types of repertoire?

This learning sequence is designed to accompany the activities in Unit 5.1 of the Student's Book, with a focus on the demands of the practical examination. Teachers will be able to dip into and out of the activities, depending on the specific learning needs of the student group. Each section has been given an approximate time frame and, where a lesson is an average of an hour in length, we anticipate that the sequence might take up to three hours or three lessons.

Learning outcomes:
- **Identify** the possibilities of different types of repertoire.
- **Explore** the idea of interpretation and apply this to a script.

Differentiated learning outcomes:
- **All** students must take part in staging activities and explore a range of different approaches to working with other actors to stage a text.
- **Most** students should shape and alter the way a scene is performed to communicate meaning to an audience.
- **Some** students could interpret a dialogue in a range of interesting ways, exploring subtext and using vocal and physical skills to create a range of meanings.

Resources:
- Student's Book: pp. 96–97
- Handout 14: Mind map template
- Handout 26: Extract from *Maria Marten – The Murder in the Red Barn*
- Handout 27: Introduction to Victorian melodrama
- Reflective Log
- Basic props for Victorian melodrama
- Flipchart or large pieces of paper and pens
- Coloured pens

Syllabus Assessment Objectives:

AO1: Understanding repertoire

Candidates will be assessed on their ability to demonstrate knowledge and understanding of the possibilities of repertoire, and how to interpret and realise it in a live performance.

AO3: Acting skills

Candidates will be assessed on their acting skills and their ability to communicate effectively to an audience.

Written work

Candidates' written answers should show practical and theoretical understanding of the play extract and devised piece they have performed as part of the course. They may need to write about a variety of aspects of:

- acting (e.g. interaction, pacing, physicality, proxemics, role, vocal expression)
- devising (e.g. characterisation, contrast, structure, tension)
- directing (e.g. advice to actors, directorial concept, mood, staging)
- design (costume and make-up, lighting, props, scenography, set, sound).

STARTING POINT (30–40 min)

Equipment: Flipchart and pens, Handout 14

➢ **Focus (10 min):** Working as a whole class, ask students to identify the key features of a dramatic script (for example, dialogue) and create a mind map on a flipchart page (use Handout 14 if appropriate).

➢ **Warm-up (10–20 min):** 'Zip, Zap, Boing!' This activity is designed to develop group awareness. It is a tried-and-tested drama game involving high-speed exchange of visual indicators.

The leader starts the game off by sending a clap around the circle with the verbal signal 'Zip!' Each player has to say 'Zip!' as they pass the clap on. Once all participants have understood this passing action, introduce the idea of 'Zap!' If you say 'Zap!' to the person who has just 'zipped' you, that sends the clap in the opposite direction.

Lastly the person that receives the 'zip' or 'zap' may choose to yell 'Boing!' and point at someone anywhere in the circle. This bounces the energy over to them. That player then restarts the clap with a 'Zip!' going in the direction of their choice. Participants are sent 'out' if they hesitate, do not contribute energy or get the direction wrong. You can also add rules – for example, you can't 'zap' a person who has just 'zapped' you.

EXPLORING THE SKILLS (30–40 min)
Equipment: Student's Book, Reflective Log

- Working as a whole class, ask students to read the short scripts extracts (A–C) on pages 96–97 of the Student's Book.
- Encourage the students to share some initial responses to the extracts (Question 1). Ask them for their first impressions of the different relationships between the characters in Extracts A and Extract B. Encourage them to come up with a range of adjectives – for example, tense, intimate, hostile.
- Ask students to break into small groups and give each group either Extract A or B to focus on. Ask the students to form a frozen tableau that reveals the relationship between the characters in their extract. As a developmental activity ask them to choose a short phrase to deliver from the tableau that tells the audience something specific about the character – for example, Cyrano might say 'tears you let fall'.
- Move on to Question 2 on page 97 of the Student's Book. Ask students to copy the comparative table into their Reflective Log. Model completion of the first row of the table and then ask students to complete the remaining two rows.

DEVELOPING THE SKILLS (20 min)
Equipment: Student's Book

- Individually or in pairs students work on Question 3, adding two or three more rows and inserting details of other texts that they have studied in the class. There are several extracts in earlier chapters of the Student's Book that they could use for this activity, including those from:
  - *The Tempest* by William Shakespeare (Caliban's speech) – Chapter 2, page 25
  - *Sparkleshark* by Philip Ridley – Chapter 2, page 29
  - *Sand Burial* – Chapter 2, page 32
  - *Red Velvet* by Lolita Chakrabarti – Chapter 2, page 35
  - *The House of Bernarda Alba* by Federico García Lorca – Chapter 3, page 42
  - *Amadeus* by Peter Shaffer – Chapter 3, pages 50–51
  - *Trojan Women* by Euripides – Chapter 3, pages 64–65
- **Option**: Students could research more plays to add to the comparative table.

APPLYING THE SKILLS (30–60 min)
Equipment: Handouts 26 and 27, Reflective Log, simple props to illustrate the melodramatic genre, computer/projector for showing clips from TV soap opera

- Explain that you are going to spend some time looking at the first of the genres listed on page 97 of the Student's Book: Victorian melodrama. Mention that these were hugely popular in the 19th century and have links to modern culture (for example, in contemporary TV drama and soap operas).
- As a whole group, read the extract from *Maria Marten – Murder in the Red Barn*, printed in Handout 26. Discuss the key features of the genre of Victorian melodrama and write a definition. (If appropriate, use Handout 27 to discuss the theatrical conventions of the English Victorian period in the 19th century.)
  - In addition, you could show a short, melodramatic scene (or set of scenes) from a modern-day soap opera to enable students to make a comparison with the contemporary style of melodrama. You could use either a soap opera the students are familiar with or one they may never have come across from another country (e.g. Brazilian telenovela) as long as the melodrama is clear.
  - Ask students to create a simple staging scenario for the scene from *Maria Marten* – use basic furniture and/or simple props to mark out the space.

- **Option**: Explore the entrances of the key characters by physically modelling their movement, gesture and posture – move from one end of the room to the other far extremity in role. Try asking students to take on a specific character and move around the room in role, interacting with other characters. They can also add a line or a few words of dialogue.
- Ask the students to consider the relationship between the actors and the audience. Taking on the role of director, work with the whole group and explore proxemics by moving the characters around the space to alter the level of intimacy / distance. Discuss the impact of moving characters closer to the audience. Develop some stock gestures for characters that will enable the audience to recognise the characters and then run the whole scene for impact.
- Review the features of melodrama and discuss the interpretation that has been created by the group.
- **Reflective Log**: Give students five minutes to record their observations, including key dramatic terms they have learned or focused on.
- **Option**: As homework, students could research the other three genres listed on page 97 of the Student's Book: comedy of the absurd, revenge drama and classical tragedy. The class could be divided into groups, with each group researching one aspect and then reporting back to the whole class with a short presentation of the genre they have investigated.

Give Extra Support: by working with an identified group of students or sets of pairs who might struggle and 'workshop' it with them. Once they have seen some possibilities, they can try it for themselves.

Challenge: students to create their own short melodramatic improvisation, using stock characters and a few lines of dialogue. More confident students can also create a script for their melodrama.

CHECKING PROGRESS	Ask students to check their progress against the progress criteria on page 97 of the Student's Book and monitor their responses, making note of whether they have reached **Sound** or **Excellent** progress.

Unit 5.2 — Interpreting the repertoire – a learning sequence

SPOTLIGHT ON:	What is interpretation and why does it matter?

This learning sequence is designed to accompany the activities in Unit 5.2 of the Student's Book, with a focus on the demands of the practical examination. Teachers will be able to dip into and out of the activities, depending on the specific learning needs of the student group. Each section has been given an approximate time frame and, where a lesson is an average of an hour in length, we anticipate that the sequence might take up to three hours or three lessons.

KEY TERMS:
interpretation

Learning outcomes:
- **Identify** the possibilities of different types of repertoire.
- **Explore** the idea of interpretation and apply this to a short script.

Differentiated learning outcomes:
- **All** students must take part in staging activities and explore a range of different approaches to working with other actors to stage a text.
- **Most** students should shape and alter the way a scene is performed to communicate meaning to an audience.
- **Some** students could interpret a dialogue in a range of interesting ways, exploring subtext and using vocal and physical skills to create a range of meanings.

Resources:
- Student's Book: pp. 98–101
- Handout 28: Extract from *Romeo and Juliet* by William Shakespeare
- Handout 29: Interpreting a dramatic text – key questions *(two copies)*
- Handout 30: Extract from *Cyrano de Bergerac* by Edmond Rostand
- Reflective Log
- Bench for staging *Cyrano* extracts
- Flipchart or a large sheet of paper and pens
- Coloured pens

Syllabus Assessment Objectives:

AO1: Understanding repertoire
Candidates will be assessed on their ability to demonstrate knowledge and understanding of the possibilities of repertoire, and how to interpret and realise it in a live performance.

AO3: Acting skills
Candidates will be assessed on their acting skills and their ability to communicate effectively to an audience.

Written work
Candidates' written answers should show practical and theoretical understanding of the play extract and devised piece they have performed as part of the course. They may need to write about a variety of aspects of:
- acting (e.g. interaction, pacing, physicality, proxemics, role, vocal expression)
- devising (e.g. characterisation, contrast, structure, tension)
- directing (e.g. advice to actors, directorial concept, mood, staging)
- design (costume and make-up, lighting, props, scenography, set, sound).

STARTING POINT (30–50 min)

Equipment: Flipchart and pens

> **Focus (10 min)**: Ask students, working as a whole class group and using the flipchart, to identify the key attributes of a dramatic character – for example, a specific action they carry out that impacts on others. Record responses in a mind map format.

> **Warm-up (10–20 min × 2)**: 'Mirroring'. This activity is designed to develop pair awareness. Ask the students to work in pairs. Start by getting the students to move to face each other so that each arm and leg is in direct mirror image. Label each person A or B, and ask A to lead their partner B by creating small movements in the mirror, which are then directly copied by partner B. If necessary, model this with two volunteers. Stress to students that the smaller the movement, the greater the accuracy of copying. Stress also the skills of communication and teamwork. After confidence has developed, ask students to swap and allow the other person to lead. Use chairs to help refine the detail in the action. Then move to standing, using space and levels, and increasing or decreasing proximity.

EXPLORING THE SKILLS (30 min)

Equipment: Student's Book

> In Question 1, on page 98 of the Student's Book, look together at the images from the so-called 'balcony scene' in *Romeo and Juliet* as a whole class, noting the key differences between them.

> For Question 2, discuss with the students the decisions made by the director to 'realise' the text. Ask them to consider various aspects of the *mise en scène* (the arrangement of scenery or stage properties in the staging of a play).

> **Option**: You could explain to students that the two photos in the Student's Book are interpretations of the famous so-called 'balcony scene' from Act II, Scene 2 of *Romeo and Juliet,* which contains the well-known lines 'O Romeo, Romeo! Wherefore art thou Romeo?' In this scene Juliet muses on her love for Romeo and the difficulties caused by the fact that they are from opposing families. Show images of other, more traditional interpretations of the scene. Ask students to work in small groups and think again about what the directors sought to achieve in the interpretations shown in the Student's Book. You could mention that in Shakespeare's play, the scene is set in Juliet's family's garden; Romeo is in the garden and the stage direction simply says: 'Juliet appears above at a window'.

DEVELOPING THE SKILLS (30–60 min)

Equipment: Student's Book, Handout 28, Handout 29

> As a whole class consider the table on page 99 of the Student's Book. Check understanding of the key terms: 'genre', 'character', 'protagonist' and 'antagonist'. Invite students to comment on the points in the table and discuss together, so that the whole group understand the important questions.

> **Option**: Distribute Handout 28 and as a whole class read the opening lines of Shakespeare's *Romeo and Juliet*. Use the blank table on Handout 29 and either complete it together as a group or, for developmental challenge, ask students to complete the table in pairs. Check students' understanding of the key terms as they apply to this text.

> **Option**: Ask students to read the plot summary for *Cyrano de Bergerac* on page 99 of the Student's Book. Then ask them whether they can tell what sort of genre the play belongs to (Question 4 on page 100).

> As a whole class read the text extract on page 100 of the Student's Book. Ask students to work in pairs to decide how they would stage the text, making notes about character as well as ideas for costume, design, lighting and sound (Questions 5 and 6). Remind them to establish the staging conventions first (for example, a bench in a garden at dusk). Ask them to complete another blank table (Handout 29) to record their thoughts and ideas. Share some of the ideas and together evaluate the staging and characterisation decisions demonstrated.

> Ask students (individually or in pairs) to read the sample student discussion in the tinted panel at the top of page 101, and work through Questions 7 and 8. Share students' ideas in the whole group.

> Describe the importance of textual annotation for actors. Draw students' attention to the modelled example on page 101 of the Student's Book. Moving on to Question 9, ask students to consider, in pairs, the level of detail that can be drawn out of a script.

APPLYING THE SKILLS (30–60 min)

Equipment: Student's Book, Handout 30, chairs for Roxanne's bench/seat, Reflective Log

- Ask students to work in the same pairs to annotate the *Cyrano* extract from page 100 with notes on their own specific interpretation. After they have spent some time on this, work through the script extract as a whole class, inviting different pairs to share examples of their notes with the whole class. Encourage the students to evaluate their annotations and decide whether they have applied enough detail and analysis to their own textual annotations, or whether they could have gone into more detail.

- **Option**: Consider a further extract from *Cyrano de Bergerac* (Handout 30). Divide students into new pairs (changing pairs around creates greater contrast in approach) and divide the script extract into small sections. (You could ask the class to help you divide the script into sections in order to promote understanding of text segmentation as a rehearsal strategy.)

- Ask students to begin by annotating their section of the script extract with ideas about character and the relationships between characters, using suitable adjectives to help express these ideas – for example, 'wistful', 'hopeful', 'sad'.

- Then ask students to plot the movement and gesture of the two characters by working through the text physically before adding the spoken dialogue.

- Finally, ask students to explore alternative options for staging – for example, they could have Cyrano sitting and Roxanne standing, or Cyrano standing and Roxanne sitting. Ask them to prepare to show their work to the rest of the class.

- As a whole class, evaluate the range of interpretations offered in terms of impact on the audience. What did they think was particularly effective?

- **Reflective Log**: Give students five minutes to record their observations including key drama terms, using the following key prompts to help: What did I do? Why did I do it? How effective was it? What did I learn?

> **Give Extra Support**: by working with an identified group of students or sets of pairs who might struggle and 'workshop' it with them. Once they have seen some possibilities, they can try it for themselves.
>
> **Challenge**: students to create their own tragic exchange between two characters in the style of *Cyrano*.

CHECKING PROGRESS	Ask students to check their progress against the progress criteria on page 101 of the Student's Book and monitor their responses, making note of whether they have reached **Sound** or **Excellent** progress.

Unit 5.3 — Exploring monologues – a learning sequence

SPOTLIGHT ON:	How can I begin to approach my monologue preparation?

This learning sequence is designed to accompany the activities in Unit 5.3 of the Student's Book, with a focus on the demands of the practical examination. Teachers will be able to dip into and out of the activities, depending on the specific learning needs of the student group. Each section has been given an approximate time frame and, where a lesson is an average of an hour in length, we anticipate that the sequence might take up to three hours or three lessons.

KEY TERMS:
monologue, blocking

Learning outcomes:
- **Investigate** factors to help choose a monologue.
- **Explore** how to develop a character.
- **Begin** structuring a monologue performance.

Differentiated learning outcomes:
- **All** students must take part in staging activities and explore a range of different approaches to staging a monologue text.
- **Most** students should shape and alter the way a monologue is performed to communicate meaning to an audience.
- **Some** students could interpret a monologue in a range of interesting ways, exploring subtext and using vocal and physical skills to create a range of meanings.

Resources:
- Student's Book: pp. 102–107
- Reflective Log
- Handout 31: Monologue comparison table
- Handout 32: Introduction to Stanislavski and 'The System'
- Chairs for assistance in staging monologue
- Flipchart or a large sheet of paper and pens
- Coloured pens
- Photocopies of the monologues on pages 103 and 104 of the Student's Book

Syllabus Assessment Objectives:

AO1: Understanding repertoire

Candidates will be assessed on their ability to demonstrate knowledge and understanding of the possibilities of repertoire, and how to interpret and realise it in a live performance.

AO3: Acting skills

Candidates will be assessed on their acting skills and their ability to communicate effectively to an audience.

Written work

Candidates' written answers should show practical and theoretical understanding of the play extract and devised piece they have performed as part of the course. They may need to write about a variety of aspects of:
- acting (e.g. interaction, pacing, physicality, proxemics, role, vocal expression)
- devising (e.g. characterisation, contrast, structure, tension)
- directing (e.g. advice to actors, directorial concept, mood, staging)
- design (costume and make-up, lighting, props, scenography, set, sound).

STARTING POINT (30–50 min)

Equipment: Flipchart or whiteboard, pens

- **Focus (10 min)**: Working as a whole class, ask students to identify the key features of a dramatic monologue. Use the flipchart to create a group mind map. Recap understanding of dramatic genre from Unit 5.1 by asking students to brainstorm the various genres where we might find a monologue.

- Read the text under 'Starting Point' on page 102 of the Student's Book.

- **Warm-up (10–20 min)**: 'Chair tango'. This activity is designed to develop pair awareness. Seat students in a circle and ask for one volunteer to stand in the centre of the circle, to be the 'lead'. You may wish to model the role of the 'lead' first, to get the game moving.

The lead person makes a statement about themselves – for example, 'I have brown hair' – and everyone for whom that statement is true, then moves across the circle to swap places with someone else. The volunteer has quickly to try to find a vacant seat while people are exchanging places, and the last one standing becomes the new lead. The statements can increase in complexity as the game moves on – for example, 'I once played saxophone in a concert', which few people will have done, thus reducing the numbers of 'tango' dancers crossing the space. This game is great for creating group energy while increasing confidence in individual students to take the 'stage' on their own, within the comfort zone of the circle.

EXPLORING THE SKILLS (30 min)

Equipment: Student's Book, Handout 31

- As a whole class, read Lucy's monologue (Monologue A) from *Invisible Friends*, on page 103 of the Student's Book. You may wish to play Lucy yourself in order to model the use of pauses (where indicated). Discuss what we have found out about Lucy and her situation. Identify the shifting emotions that Lucy displays as she talks to her invisible friend Zara. Discuss the staging challenges represented by the setting of a teenage girl's bedroom.

- In pairs students should now read Monologue B: Valere from *La Bête* (Student's Book page 104). As a whole group discuss Questions 2 and 3 in the Student's Book, gathering first impressions and thinking about the structure and layout of the monologues. Ask what the main differences in style and language are between the two monologues.

- Ask students, in their pairs, to complete the comparison table on Handout 31 and check answers with the rest of the group. Discuss the main challenges of performing a monologue to the audience or other actors (e.g. holding attention, introducing variety, using appropriate pause and stillness).

DEVELOPING THE SKILLS (30–60 min)

Equipment: Student's Book, photocopies of the monologues on pages 103 and 104 of the Student's Book, A1 paper and pens, chair for hot-seating

- As a whole class consider the characterisation diagram on page 106 of the Student's Book. Check understanding of the key terms: 'physicality', 'gait', 'pitch', 'period', 'tone', 'accent'. You may wish physically to model some of the terms (e.g. gait, pitch) or ask some volunteers to do so for you.

- Ask students to work in pairs, with one student acting as actor and another as director. Ask them to choose to work on either Monologue A or Monologue B. They should now work on creating their own characterisation diagram, using paper and marker pens so that ideas are clearly visible. You may need to model a few of the branches on the diagram so that students understand what is required.

- **Option**: Demonstrate or recap the skill of hot-seating by taking on a fictional role and seating yourself in front of the class. Encourage students to use the categories on the characterisation diagram to ask questions of the character: for example, How many people are there in your family? Explain that any extra detail that emerges from the hot-seating exercise can be added to the diagram. Ask students to hot-seat the character in their pairs.

- **Option**: Students can now choose to work on a specific section of the monologue – no more than one half of the text. Discuss the example of annotation given in the Student's Book (and practised in Unit 5.2) and ask students to annotate the text (using photocopies of the relevant page) to indicate their ideas for staging, including movement, physicality, posture, gesture, facial expression, and so on.

APPLYING THE SKILLS (30–60 min)

Equipment: Reflective Log, Handout 32, chairs for staging

➢ Students can now try to stage the whole monologue, using one partner as the director and the other as the performer. They can adjust their annotation as they work. If appropriate, you could ask them to clearly identify their characters' 'through-line' or 'super-objective' (as outlined in Handout 32 on Stanislavski's 'System', which you will have introduced in Unit 2.1. **Option**: If you haven't used this handout before, you could spend some time here looking at Stanislavski's ideas and how they can be used to help in developing a character).

You can encourage the students to try different positions for the audience – for example, end-on staging, thrust, in-the-round – and evaluate the impact of each. Watch a selection of these and discuss the impact of staging and performance decisions.

➢ **Option**: If the students are ready for a developmental challenge you might ask them to experiment with the genre of the piece – for example, playing Lucy's monologue as if she is in a Victorian melodrama, or Valere as if he is in a modern-day soap opera. You could give each pair a different genre to try or, more simply, just ask them to experiment with pace and tone. You could try using a metronome to alter the pace.

➢ **Reflective Log**: Give students five minutes to record their observations, including key dramatic terms, using the following key prompts to help: What did I do? Why did I do it? How effective was it? What did I learn?

Give Extra Support: by working with an identified group of students or sets of pairs who might struggle and 'workshop' it with them. Once they have seen some possibilities, they can try it for themselves.

Challenge: more confident students to create their own tragic or comic monologues and stage them for an audience.

CHECKING PROGRESS	Ask students to check their progress against the progress criteria on page 107 of the Student's Book and monitor their responses, making note of whether they have reached **Sound** or **Excellent** progress.

Unit 5.4 — Exploring group scripts – a learning sequence

SPOTLIGHT ON:	How can my group rehearse our script effectively?

This learning sequence is designed to accompany the activities in Unit 5.4 of the Student's Book, with a focus on the demands of the practical examination. Teachers will be able to dip into and out of the activities, depending on the specific learning needs of the student group. Each section has been given an approximate time frame and, where a lesson is an average of an hour in length, we anticipate that the sequence might take up to three hours or three lessons.

KEY TERMS:
subtext

Learning outcomes:
- **Identify** approaches to exploring and rehearsing an extract for performance.
- **Explore** ways to shape scenes and interact on stage, developing meaning and impact.

Differentiated learning outcomes:
- **All** students must take part in staging activities and explore a range of different approaches to working with other actors to stage a text.
- **Most** students should shape and alter the way a scene is performed to communicate meaning to an audience.
- **Some** students could interpret a dialogue in a range of interesting ways, exploring subtext and using vocal and physical skills to create a range of meanings.

Resources:
- Student's Book: pp. 108–115
- Reflective Log
- Handout 14: Mind map template
- Handout 24: Drawing ground plans
- Handout 33: Introduction to Georgian society and theatre
- Flipchart or A1 paper and pens
- Coloured pens
- Range of text extracts including poems, novel extracts, news articles
- Selected props – ribbons to act as bindings for King George, chair on wheels
- Copies of the extract on pages 109–111 of the Student's Book

Syllabus Assessment Objectives:

AO1: Understanding repertoire

Candidates will be assessed on their ability to demonstrate knowledge and understanding of the possibilities of repertoire, and how to interpret and realise it in a live performance.

AO3: Acting skills

Candidates will be assessed on their acting skills and their ability to communicate effectively to an audience.

Written work

Candidates' written answers should show practical and theoretical understanding of the play extract and devised piece they have performed as part of the course. They may need to write about a variety of aspects of:
- acting (e.g. interaction, pacing, physicality, proxemics, role, vocal expression)
- devising (e.g. characterisation, contrast, structure, tension)
- directing (e.g. advice to actors, directorial concept, mood, staging)
- design (costume and make-up, lighting, props, scenography, set, sound).

STARTING POINT (30 min)

Equipment: Student's Book, A1 paper and pens and a range of different text extracts of the teacher's choice, Handout 14

- **Focus (15 min)**: Examine the differences between scripts, novels and poems by creating three separate visual mind maps (divide the group into three or discuss as one group). Use the mind map template in Handout 14 if appropriate.

- **Warm-up (10–20 min)**: The following warm-up activities are designed to develop group awareness. Run one or both depending on the needs of the group.

- 'Tectonic plates' – Ask your group simply to walk around the space moving towards a specific destination and then when they reach that point to change direction. They should aim to avoid a circular crowd-like movement. Then ask the group to imagine that the floor of the space is balanced on a central pivot; as they move around the space they have to maintain the floor's balance. They must keep moving (calmly, not running) and look for empty spaces to fill. When any spaces become filled by someone else, they must find a new empty space. Weaving in and out of each other, heading in all directions, they will gradually begin to anticipate where empty spaces may open up. This will help them to develop a heightened sense of awareness of the rest of the group and their movements in the space.

- **Option**: 'Impulses' – While students are walking around the space, provide the group with a variety of instructions. They should react immediately to each instruction as quickly as possible. This exercise will develop focus, awareness, listening skills and impulsive reactions to instructions. The following can offer a starting point:

    - 'Wall!' – run and place both hands on the wall
    - 'Centre!' – gather in the centre of the room
    - 'Jump!' – jump once then continue walking
    - 'Floor!' – touch both hands on the floor, then continue walking
    - 'Stop!' – stand still.

- Ask students to read through the bullet points in 'Starting point' on page 108 of the Student's Book, and make sure they understand the meaning of 'subtext'.

- In answering Question 1, students should share their experiences, if any, of working on group scripts. Ask for examples of what they found challenging and difficult, as well as what they found went well.

EXPLORING THE SKILLS (60 min)

Equipment: Student's Book, Handout 33, Reflective Log, computers / internet access for research, flipchart or whiteboard, pens

- Give students a few minutes to read, individually, the extract from the script in the Student's Book, on pages 109–111.

- Share some initial responses to the script, as suggested in Question 4 on page 112 of the Student's Book. Ask the group for their first impressions of the different status of various characters and the tensions between them. Discuss the concept of divine monarchy: this is the once common belief that the monarch is chosen, appointed and ordained by God to rule, and is therefore above question or challenge, and is not accountable to their subjects, only to God. Introduce a definition on a whiteboard or flipchart.

- Ask the students to work together to answer Question 3 on page 112 of the Student's Book, researching some key aspects of the content of the play, such as its historical, political and social context. Students should then share in groups or as a whole class. **Option**: If helpful, you can provide copies of Handout 33, which gives information about Georgian society and theatre.

- **Reflective Log**: Give students five minutes to reflect on their contribution to these activities using the questions: What did I do? Why did I do it? What did I learn?

DEVELOPING THE SKILLS (60 min)

Equipment: Student's Book, Reflective Log

- Give students 5–10 minutes to reread the text extract on pages 109–111 of the Student's Book as a group and set aside plenty of time for them to try Questions 5–7 on pages 112–114 of the Student's Book.

- As a whole group break the scene down into units of action (moment from the text where something specific takes place) and draw dividing lines where each unit starts (there should be approximately four).

- Ask students to form frozen tableaux for the scene that reveals where the various members of the family might stand in relation to one another. Use 'forum theatre' to swap actors into and out of the picture and experiment with levels and posture. (**Note**: 'Forum Theatre' was developed by Augusto Boal. It is a type of theatre whereby actors or audience members can stop a performance, in which a character is being oppressed in some way. The audience can suggest different actions for the actors to carry out on-stage in an attempt to change the outcome of what they are seeing. In 'Forum Theatre' audience members may be asked to come on stage and perform their own interventions.) Try adding a newspaper caption (or phrase that goes with a photo) to describe the relationships in the family and ask one of the actors to include it in the image by speaking it out loud at the point of the freeze, for example 'Happy families!'.

- **Reflective Log**: Give students five minutes to write up their observations, focusing on the questions: What did I do and why did I do it?

APPLYING THE SKILLS (60 min)

Equipment: Student's Book, copies of the extract on pages 109–111 of the Student's Book, Handout 24, Reflective Log, A1 paper and coloured pens, flipchart or whiteboard

- Divide the students into small groups to answer Question 8 on page 114 of the Student's Book. It might be useful to provide a floor plan for a proscenium arch theatre on which students can draw a box set design (simple plan showing any theatrical scenery, entrances and exits, any furniture and theatre wings) for a production of the play (use Handout 24 if helpful here).

- Give students a set of coloured pens and ask them to use colours to track the movements of the different characters in the extract. Allocate one colour per character. Drawing on the previous tableaux activity, discuss the impact of movement on the shifting status of the characters. Who moves the most and what does this say about the power of the king?

- Allocate each group one of the units of action to work on: for example, when the king is strapped into the chair.

- For Question 9, use the extract from pages 109–111. Ask the students to identify 10 key words from the dialogue that express the relationships between characters. They should then use the tracking diagram to begin to plot interactions between characters, using the key words to annotate each movement on the script. Students should annotate the possible movements of the character, for example 'turns slowly'. You may need to model this activity using the section of text given on page 114 of the Student's Book.

- **Option**: Ask each group to explore the text in practical terms, experimenting with pace and tone by speeding up or slowing down delivery of the lines to emphasise shifting power relationships. After five minutes of experimentation, introduce the concept of subtext by writing it on the flipchart or whiteboard. Ask each group to write a 'what's really going on?' statement on their text extract.

- Next ask each group to add appropriate facial expression, posture and gesture for each character to express the subtext.

- Ask for two volunteers to demonstrate examples to illustrate the difference between what is said and what is not said. Ask them to perform part of the extract, focusing on the impact of blocking, physicality and facial expression. Analyse the performance with the group, focusing on gesture and facial expression, and how these convey the meaning to an audience.

- Finally, the class should put on a complete performance of the script – with different groups taking over at various points, performing their own 'unit of action' that they have worked on.

- **Reflective Log**: Give students 5–10 minutes to record their observations and reflections on these extended activities, including key dramatic terms.

Give Extra Support: by working with an identified group of students or sets of pairs who might struggle and 'workshop' it with them. Once they have seen some possibilities, they can try it for themselves.

Challenge: students to 'put the text back' by wrapping dialogue around their key words – without losing clarity in movement and interaction.

CHECKING PROGRESS	Ask students to check their progress against the progress criteria on page 115 of the Student's Book and monitor their responses, making note of whether they have reached **Sound** or **Excellent** progress.

Unit 5.5 — Applying the skills – a learning sequence

SPOTLIGHT ON:	How do I bring all my script performance skills together?

This learning sequence is designed to accompany the activities in Unit 5.5 of the Student's Book, with a focus on the demands of the practical examination. Teachers will be able to dip into and out of the activities, depending on the specific learning needs of the student group. Each section has been given an approximate time frame and, where a lesson is an average of an hour in length, we anticipate that the sequence might take up to three hours or three lessons.

Learning outcomes:
- **Identify** the ways of bringing a range of dramatic skills together to perform a monologue.
- **Explore** the idea of interpretation and apply this to a script.

Differentiated learning outcomes:
- **All** students must take part in staging activities and explore a range of different approaches to staging a monologue text.
- **Most** students should shape and alter the way a monologue is performed to communicate meaning to an audience.
- **Some** students could interpret a monologue in a range of interesting ways, exploring subtext and using vocal and physical skills to create a range of meanings.

Resources:
- Student's Book: pp. 116–117
- Reflective Log
- Handout 22: Role on the wall
- Handout 32: Introduction to Stanislavski and 'The System'
- Fabric blindfolds
- Chairs for assistance in staging monologue
- Flipchart or A1 paper and pens
- Coloured pens

Syllabus Assessment Objectives:

AO1: Understanding repertoire

Candidates will be assessed on their ability to demonstrate knowledge and understanding of the possibilities of repertoire, and how to interpret and realise it in a live performance.

AO3: Acting skills

Candidates will be assessed on their acting skills and their ability to communicate effectively to an audience.

Written work

Candidates' written answers should show practical and theoretical understanding of the play extract and devised piece they have performed as part of the course. They may need to write about a variety of aspects of:
- acting (e.g. interaction, pacing, physicality, proxemics, role, vocal expression)
- devising (e.g. characterisation, contrast, structure, tension)
- directing (e.g. advice to actors, directorial concept, mood, staging)
- design (costume and make-up, lighting, props, scenography, set, sound).

STARTING POINT (30 min)

Equipment: Student's Book, Handout 22, flipchart and pens / whiteboard

> **Focus (10 min)**: Working as a whole class group and using the flipchart, ask students to create a group 'role on the wall' (see Handout 22 for a template) for Cyrano (encountered in Unit 5.2 – see page 100 of the Student's Book). They should record all of the characteristics of Cyrano, as seen by others, on the outside of the figure and all those that he experiences himself on the inside.

- **Warm-up (10–20 min)**: 'Blindfold song'. This activity is designed to develop sensitivity to a range of stimuli. Ask students to work in pairs and label themselves A and B. The pairs need to agree on a simple song or lullaby that they both know.
- Ask student A to blindfold student B or ask student B to close their eyes. Student A then moves at least 2 metres away from Student B and guides them around the room by singing the song they have agreed. Student B should follow simply by locating where the sound of the agreed song is coming from. Student A should take care to guide Student B around obstacles and away from walls.
- After a few minutes the pairs can swap roles. The exercise should help the pairs to develop spatial awareness and active listening, which are both key to strong performance skills.

EXPLORING THE SKILLS (30 min)

Equipment: Student's Book

- As a whole class group, read Walter's monologue (from *A Raisin in the Sun*) reproduced on page 116 of the Student's Book. You may wish to play Walter in order to model the use of pauses. Discuss the potential audience for Walter's monologue.

DEVELOPING THE SKILLS (30–60 min)

Equipment: Student's Book, A1 paper and pens, chair for hot-seating

- Ask the group to work in pairs on Question 2 on page 117 of the Student's Book, creating a spider diagram for the character of Walter. Refer back to the example spider diagram on page 106 in Unit 5.3. You may need to model a few of the branches on the diagram so that students understand what is required.
- Seat the class in a hot-seating format. Encourage students to use the categories on the characterisation diagram to ask questions of the character: for example, Where were you born? Where did you grow up? How many people are there in your family? Explain that any extra detail that emerges from the hot-seating exercise can be added to the diagram. Ask students to hot-seat the character in their pairs.
- **Option**: Check understanding of the key terms in the example spider diagram: 'physicality', 'gait', 'period', 'tone', 'pitch', 'accent'. Ask students to work in pairs with one student acting as actor and another as director. Students can now choose to work on a specific section of the monologue – no more than one half of the text. Discuss the example of annotation given on page 117 of the Student's Book (and also practised in previous units – for example, on pages 107 and 114) and ask students to annotate the text to indicate their ideas for staging including movement, physicality, posture, gesture, facial expression (Question 3).

APPLYING THE SKILLS (30–60 min)

Equipment: Student's Book, Handout 32, Reflective Log, chairs for staging, metronome

- Students can now try to stage the whole monologue with one partner being the director and the other being the performer. They can adjust their annotation in the light of how well things work and what could be changed. They should be able to clearly identify the character's motivations and emotions (use Handout 32 on Stanislavski and 'The System', if helpful). You can encourage the students to try different positions for the audience – for example, end-on staging, thrust, or in-the-round – and to evaluate the impact of the different positions.
- Watch a selection of students' monologues and, as a whole group, discuss the impact of staging and performance decisions.
- **Option**: If students are ready for a developmental challenge, ask them to experiment with the genre of the piece – for example, playing the monologue as if Walter is in a TV soap opera or an American Western. You could give each pair a different genre to try or, more simply, just ask them to experiment with pace and tone. You could try using a metronome to alter the rhythm and pace of students' delivery.
- **Reflective Log**: Give students a few minutes to record their reflections on this section, including application of key dramatic terms and using the following key prompts to help: What did I do? Why did I do it? How effective was it? What did I learn?

Give Extra Support: by working with an identified group of students or sets of pairs who might struggle and 'workshop' it with them. Once they have seen some possibilities, they can try it for themselves.

Challenge: more confident students to write their own tragic or comic monologues and stage them for an audience.

| CHECKING PROGRESS | Ask students to check their progress against the progress criteria on page 117 of the Student's Book and monitor their responses, making note of whether they have reached **Sound** or **Excellent** progress. |

Unit 6.1 — Exploring a longer script – a learning sequence

SPOTLIGHT ON:	How can I break down a longer script so that I can engage with its ideas and structures?

This learning sequence is designed to accompany the activities in Unit 6.1 of the Student's Book, with a focus on the demands of the practical examination. Teachers will be able to dip into and out of the activities, depending on the specific learning needs of the student group. Each section has been given an approximate time frame and, where a lesson is an average of an hour in length, we anticipate that the sequence might take up to three hours or three lessons.

KEY TERMS:
motif, dynamic

Learning outcomes:
- **Identify** possible approaches and interpretations when working on a longer script.
- **Understand** how the role can link to the overall concept.

Differentiated learning outcomes:
- **All** students must focus on specific elements within a longer script and develop different skills to address them.
- **Most** students should express their ideas for staging a text in written as well as practical formats.
- **Some** students could employ peer-assessment strategies to read and evaluate written responses to a longer script.

Resources:
- Student's Book: pp. 120–125
- Reflective Log
- Handout 32: Introduction to Stanislavski and 'The System'
- Handout 34: *Humble Boy* characterisation table
- Flipchart or large piece of paper and pens
- Coloured pens

Syllabus Assessment Objectives:

AO1: Understanding repertoire

Candidates will be assessed on their ability to demonstrate knowledge and understanding of the possibilities of repertoire, and how to interpret and realise it in a live performance.

AO3: Acting skills

Candidates will be assessed on their acting skills and their ability to communicate effectively to an audience.

Written work

Candidates' written answers should show practical and theoretical understanding of the play extract and devised piece they have performed as part of the course. They may need to write about a variety of aspects of:
- acting (e.g. interaction, pacing, physicality, proxemics, role, vocal expression)
- devising (e.g. characterisation, contrast, structure, tension)
- directing (e.g. advice to actors, directorial concept, mood, staging)
- design (costume and make-up, lighting, props, scenography, set, sound).

STARTING POINT (20–30 min)

Equipment: Student's Book, computers / projector with internet access

- **Focus (10 min)**: Students should be introduced to the idea of a motif by considering the imagery on the poster for the original *Blade Runner* movie (look on the internet for this, in colour). Ask them to spend three minutes in pairs looking for and noting the dominant images and recurring ideas in the poster. Use the feedback to explain the concept of a recurring motif in drama and film.

- **Warm-up (10–20 min)**: 'Elemental stretch'. This activity is designed to develop a sense of physical awareness in the performer. Introduce the conceptual framework of the four elements of 'Earth, Fire, Air and Water'. Ask students to stand with their feet planted on the ground hip width apart, becoming aware of any tension in the shoulders. Ask them to roll their shoulders to gently release tension and ensure that their eyeline is comfortably straight ahead.

    - Earth – Ask students to float their arms upwards towards waist height and ensure that they are taut. Ask them to stretch across to two walls of the room with feet still planted on the 'earth'.
    - Fire – Second, and with feet in the same position, they take their arms towards the ceiling with palms facing inwards and stretch onto the toes of the feet – 'fire'.
    - Water – Next, they roll down from the top of the head, vertebra by vertebra, with arms floating down to the ground and knees gently bent, to create a 'waterfall'. They roll back up slowly and bring shoulders and head back to normal standing position.
    - Air – Finally, they rotate both arms towards one another and towards the body, making a full circle and gently floating the arms back towards the body – 'air'.

- As a whole class, discuss what key ideas or themes we sometimes see emerging in plays (e.g. loss, regret, power, longing). Explain that it is important to try to identify what key ideas or themes are contained within a play, and that sometimes motifs are used as a device (or tool) to communicate those key ideas. Look at the definition of motif on page 120 of the Student's Book and discuss it together.

- As a class, read the background information about *Humble Boy* on page 120 ('The context of the play') and the information on the 'Set' on pages 120–121, in the blue panel before the dialogue begins. Ask students to work in groups of three if possible, to read the extract from pages 121–123.

- Students read the extract in their groups. While reading, they should try to identify key ideas or themes emerging. Ask them to note down any key ideas or themes.

EXPLORING THE SKILLS (30–60 min)

Equipment: Student's Book, Reflective Log, Handout 34

- Help students to identify and discuss the main ideas in the extract, reading through the points set out at the bottom of page 123.

- With students working individually or in pairs, ask them to answer Question 2, on page 124 of the Student's Book, writing sentences about key ideas and motifs. Then share their sentences a whole class.

- Distribute the table set out on page 124 and reproduced in Handout 34. Students should work individually or in pairs to complete it. As they work through Questions 4, 5 and 6, finish this section with a class discussion on dynamics. Discuss and explain the key definition of dynamic. Ask students to find examples of the dynamics between characters in the script.

- **Reflective Log**: Students should write some initial notes on how this scene from *Humble Boy* might be played. Ask the students to complete the challenge task in the table from Handout 34, and include it in their Reflective Log.

DEVELOPING THE SKILLS (30–60 min)

Equipment: Student's Book, Reflective Log, flipchart or whiteboard, pens

- As a whole group re-read the opening exchange between Mercy and Felix. With a volunteer, model the tennis match technique where the two performers stand on opposite sides of a fictional net and send the lines of dialogue across the net towards one another, miming the use of a tennis racket. The level of status that the character has will determine who wins the fictional shot. Discuss the changing dynamics between the characters and how this might affect the actors' physicality.

- Ask students, in pairs, to experiment with proxemics and movement between the two characters in this extract. Use the points in Questions 7 and 8 on page 125 in the Student's Book to steer this activity.

- **Option**: Perform a couple of examples from the script and discuss status, gesture, facial expression and vocal skills. Check that students can answer the following questions:
  - How do the two actors demonstrate the motherly relationship that Mercy has with Felix?
  - How is Felix's grief demonstrated?

  Record students' answer on a flipchart or whiteboard and annotate the text with ideas for physical and vocal performance skills.
- **Reflective Log**: Ask students to write a short paragraph in response to the two questions.

APPLYING THE SKILLS (30–60 min)
Equipment: Student's Book, Handout 32, Reflective Log

- Ask students to work in groups of four, where the fourth person takes on the role of director. Instruct them to annotate the script with a Stanislavskian overarching objective for each character – for example, Felix: 'to persuade others of the extent of the loss of my father'. This can be called the super-objective. Use Handout 32, which gives brief definitions of each of Stanislavski's key terms. Ask students to attach an active verb (as described in Handout 32) and a specific set of actions that will help the actors to develop a role in this extract.
- Students should then rehearse the extract, playing the specific verb-led actions – for example, for Mercy it could be 'to comfort', with appropriate soothing hand gestures and sympathetic facial expressions.
- Ask students to perform and evaluate their work on proxemics and characterisation. Reinforce the use of key drama vocabulary, such as 'posture', 'gesture', 'pitch'.
- **Reflective Log**: Ask students to make notes about what they have achieved in this unit, in particular on their work as an actor in the development of character.

> **Give Extra Support**: by helping students to work through specific objectives for each character in the text.
>
> **Challenge**: students to create a ground plan for a set design for the play *Humble Boy*. (**Option**: use selected pages from Handout 24 to assist students.)

CHECKING PROGRESS	Ask students to check their progress against the progress criteria on page 125 of the Student's Book and monitor their responses, making note of whether they reached **Sound** or **Excellent** progress.

| Unit 6.2 | **Responding to specific aspects of the script – a learning sequence** |

| **SPOTLIGHT ON:** | How can I tackle tasks that require me to focus on very specific parts of a script? |

This learning sequence is designed to accompany the activities in Unit 6.2 of the Student's Book, with a focus on the demands of the practical examination. Teachers will be able to dip into and out of the activities, depending on the specific learning needs of the student group. Each section has been given an approximate time frame and, where a lesson is an average of an hour in length, we anticipate that the sequence might take up to three hours or three lessons.

Learning outcomes:
- **Identify** possible approaches and interpretations when working on a longer script.
- **Explore** how performance, design or directorial decisions can impact on the interpretation of a dramatic script.

Differentiated learning outcomes:
- **All** students must focus on specific elements within a longer script and develop different skills to address them.
- **Most** students should express their ideas for staging a text in written as well as practical formats.
- **Some** students could employ peer assessment strategies to read and evaluate written responses to a longer script.

Resources:
- Student's Book: pp. 126–129
- Reflective Log
- Handout 35: 'I Love the Daffodils'
- Handout 32, Introduction to Stanislavski and 'The System'
- Selected props for Focus activity (tea tray with items for tea, garden rake, photo of Felix's father, funeral urn) or a set of cards labelled with these items to act as symbolic replacements
- Photocopies of the *Humble Boy* extract from pages 120–123 of the Student's Book
- Photocopies of the short extract between Felix and Flora from page 128 of the Student's Book
- Flipchart or A1 paper and pens
- Coloured pens

Syllabus Assessment Objectives:

AO1: Understanding repertoire

Candidates will be assessed on their ability to demonstrate knowledge and understanding of the possibilities of repertoire, and how to interpret and realise it in a live performance.

AO3: Acting skills

Candidates will be assessed on their acting skills and their ability to communicate effectively to an audience.

Written work

Candidates' written answers should show practical and theoretical understanding of the play extract and devised piece they have performed as part of the course. They may need to write about a variety of aspects of:
- acting (e.g. interaction, pacing, physicality, proxemics, role, vocal expression)
- devising (e.g. characterisation, contrast, structure, tension)
- directing (e.g. advice to actors, directorial concept, mood, staging)
- design (costume and make-up, lighting, props, scenography, set, sound).

STARTING POINT (30–40 min)

Equipment: Student's Book, Handout 35, selected props (tea tray with items for tea, garden rake, photo of Felix's father, funeral urn) or a set of cards labelled with these items to act as symbolic replacements

- **Focus (20 min)**: Ask students to form a circle with a selection of props for the extract from *Humble Boy* (pages 120–123 of the Student's Book) placed in the centre. One volunteer moves into the centre and adopts a starting pose for Felix, using one of the props. Another volunteer joins him as Mercy. The group discuss the impact of choice of props on the dynamic between the characters. The exercise is repeated until all of the props have been used. Discuss the impact of props on changing use of space, gesture, posture and physicality. As an extension ask students to suggest and, if possible, introduce alternative props.

- **Warm-up (10–20 min)**: 'I Love the Daffodils'. This activity is designed to help students to develop vocal characterisation. Use this song, detailed on Handout 35, to develop choral singing and confidence in matching song with gesture. You can find recordings of the song online (look on YouTube). Once the group has a developed understanding of the words and the tune, you can put the students into small groups and create a canon movement for the song – singing it in three or four groups as a 'round', where each group comes in to the song after two lines (or four beats – after the word 'daffodils').

EXPLORING THE SKILLS (30–60 min)

Equipment: Student's Book

- As a whole class students read the sample paragraph written by a student in response to the use of props (page 127 of the Student's Book). Discuss Questions 3 and 4 that follow, focusing on the effectiveness of the analysis.

- Introduce the three different possible roles of a prop, given in the table on page 127: functional, atmospheric and symbolic. Make sure that students understand the different purposes.

- Ask students, in pairs, to re-read the extract from *Humble Boy* (pages 120–123) and annotate it with all of the possible props that might be used. Draw students' attention to the sample props list at the bottom of page 127, but encourage them to think of more.

- Ask students to choose one of the props from their final list and write a paragraph explaining what the prop is, who could use it, and how it might be used for dramatic impact (Question 5).

DEVELOPING THE SKILLS (30–60 min)

Equipment: Student's Book, photocopies of the *Humble Boy* extract, Reflective Log, Handout 32, highlighter pens

- As a whole group re-read the short exchange between Felix and Flora on page 128 of the Student's Book. Discuss the contrast between the two characters and the possible reasons for Flora's anger. If necessary, explain that a 'Cambridge don' – Flora's description of her son – is a senior academic at Cambridge University, so refers to someone very clever. Try to steer students towards understanding the sarcasm and frustration in Flora's words, if they haven't picked up on that.

- Ask students to work in small groups of three or four to improvise the possible actions that the characters might have been engaging in before this scene, giving a couple of examples – for example, Flora might have been socialising with family and friends at her husband's wake, or Felix might have been sitting on his own biting his nails, nervously. Show a couple of example scenes and, in response to the improvisation, discuss the Stanislavskian super-objective for each character in the specified extract (refer to Handout 32 if necessary).

- Ask students to work through Question 6 on page 128, focusing on Flora's tone of voice (full of exasperation and sarcasm), her emphasis on particular words (probably: 'carry', 'lacking', 'waiting', 'church', 'you', 'just', 'right', 'clever', 'golden', 'Cambridge don', 'father's oration'), her body language (her posture and facial expressions).

- **Option**: Return to the script and focus on the vocal skills of the actors by identifying some of the words that would be emphasised. Students can continue to work through the extract and identify all of the key words. Using the first two pages of the extract, ask students to work through 'punctuation shift' by taking on a specific character and starting to walk around the space, changing direction every time there is a change of punctuation. This exercise helps to highlight the level of emotion and agitation in the dialogue.

- In Question 7, students practise the short exchange again, drawing on the points they have been considering.

- Refer students to the description of one student's ideas about how Flora's speech should be performed (top of page 129), encouraging them to analyse and evaluate it. Ask them to work through Questions 8 and 9.

- In Questions 10 and 11, students should work individually or in pairs to write their own paragraph. (The student's description should perhaps have included something about Flora's posture and body language. The description mentions Flora's gritted teeth, but more information on her facial expression and gestures would have been useful, as would a mention of possible props.)

- **Option**: Ask students to write notes in their Reflective Log on their vocal characterisation work. If necessary, give them a short series of prompt questions, such as:
    - What sort of tone of voice would you expect your character to adopt?
    - What sort of language does the character use?
    - What are the key words?
    - How do vocal skills affect physicality, including facial expression, movement and gesture?

APPLYING THE SKILLS (30–60 min)

Equipment: Student's Book, photocopies of the short extract between Felix and Flora (page 128 of the Student's Book)

- In Question 12 on page 129, students should work in pairs and allocate the roles of Felix and Mercy. Ask them to use their skills in vocal and physical characterisation to rehearse the particular exchange between the two characters. Ask them to experiment with use of space, levels, props, tone of voice and movement. Ask them to decide on a verb that describes Mercy's super-objective.

- When students have rehearsed, choose a few of the pairs to perform the short piece to the rest of the class. Invite students to give constructive comments, so that the various interpretations of the same lines can be compared and contrasted.

- **Option**: Students should write a short summative statement for the character of Mercy. They should describe how they would develop the character in the play, commenting on tone of voice, gestures, movement and facial expression. Encourage them to add comments on props and costume, and reflect on the key relationships Mercy forms in the play.

Give Extra Support: by working with students to develop freeze frames that clarify relationships, status and objectives. Support the highlighting of key words and discuss the impact of vocal emphasis by modelling different tones of voice.

Challenge: students to script the preceding improvised scene from the play *Humble Boy*.

CHECKING PROGRESS	Ask students to check their progress against the progress criteria on page 129 of the Student's Book and monitor their responses, making note of whether they have reached **Sound** or **Excellent** progress.

Unit 6.3 Writing extended responses – a learning sequence

| SPOTLIGHT ON: | How can I write a sustained response on a longer script? |

This learning sequence is designed to accompany the activities in Unit 6.3 of the Student's Book with a focus on the demands of the practical examination. Teachers will be able to dip into and out of the activities depending on the specific learning needs of the student group. Each section has been given an approximate time frame and where a lesson is an average of an hour in length, we anticipate that the sequence might take up to three hours or three lessons.

Learning outcomes:
- **Express** detailed ideas about acting design or directorial vision.
- **Understand** how performance, design or directorial decisions can impact on the interpretation of a dramatic script.

Differentiated learning outcomes:
- **All** students must focus on specific elements within a longer script and develop different skills to address them.
- **Most** students should be able to express their ideas for staging a text in written as well as practical formats.
- **Some** students could employ peer assessment strategies to read and evaluate written responses to a longer script.

Resources:
- Student's Book: pp. 130–133
- Handout 22: Role on the wall (enlarged onto A1 paper)
- Handout 32: Introduction to Stanislavski and 'The System'
- Handout 36: Characterisation table for Felix
- Handout 37: Units and objectives for *Humble Boy*
- Copies of Scene 2 of *Humble Boy*
- Flipchart or a large piece of paper and pens
- Coloured pens
- Reflective Log

Syllabus Assessment Objectives:

AO1: Understanding repertoire

Candidates will be assessed on their ability to demonstrate knowledge and understanding of the possibilities of repertoire, and how to interpret and realise it in a live performance.

AO3: Acting skills

Candidates will be assessed on their acting skills and their ability to communicate effectively to an audience.

Written work

Candidates' written answers should show practical and theoretical understanding of the play extract and devised piece they have performed as part of the course. They may need to write about a variety of aspects of:
- acting (e.g. interaction, pacing, physicality, proxemics, role, vocal expression)
- devising (e.g. characterisation, contrast, structure, tension)
- directing (e.g. advice to actors, directorial concept, mood, staging)
- design (costume and make-up, lighting, props, scenography, set, sound).

STARTING POINT (30–40 min)

Equipment: Student's Book, Handout 22 (enlarged onto A1 paper)

➢ **Focus (20 min)**: In this activity, students will focus on the development of characterisation for Felix in the play *Humble Boy*. Using the 'role on the wall' (provided on Handout 22 and enlarged onto A1 paper), ask students to work in pairs to annotate what they think Felix is thinking and feeling inside the figure and how others see him around the outside of the figure. Share ideas as a whole group.

➢ **Warm-up (10–20 min)**: 'Child's play'. This activity is designed to help students to develop physical characterisation skills. Ask students to visualise a photograph of Felix as a young child – what is the child doing? Imagine him at school in a 'play' session. Would he sit on his own? Is he shy, or confident and chatty? Would he share toys?

Ask students to move into a space on their own and pick up an imaginary toy to play with, as if they were a young version of Felix. After they have had two minutes playing with the imaginary toy, ask them to begin to notice other 'children'. How does Felix as a child get on with other children? Ask students to notice the impact of integration on their own facial expression, movements and gestures.

From their position on the ground, draw them up to a standing position, using a count of 1 to 10, where 10 represents their character growing into an adult. Ask students to move around the space in role as Felix noticing any remnants of their childhood self in their physicality and facial expression.

EXPLORING THE SKILLS (30–60 min)

Equipment: Student's Book, Handout 36, Reflective Log

➢ Ask the students to re-read the extract from *Humble Boy* (pages 120–123 of the Student's Book), this time focusing on the character of Felix. Read the notes written into the table on pages 130–131 of the Student's Book. Ask students to complete the second column of the table, using Handout 36. They could work in pairs before sharing their ideas with the whole class.

➢ **Reflective Log:** Ask the students to complete Question 3 on page 131, writing a short summary paragraph that conveys what Felix is like as a character, and include it in their Reflective Log.

DEVELOPING THE SKILLS (30–60 min)

Equipment: Student's Book, Reflective Log, Handout 32, Handout 36, Handout 37, music player and speakers

➢ As a whole class, read the paragraph under the heading 'Developing the skills' on page 131 of the

Student's Book. Discuss the link between stage directions and characterisation. What clues do the stage directions give that help with vocal skills, gesture, proxemics, facial expression, movement and so on? Then ask students to complete the third column of the table on Handout 36.

➢ Look at the table on page 132 of the Student's Book, which breaks down Felix's journey in this scene of the play into a series of phases or units. Use Handout 32 to remind students of the usefulness of Stanislavski's units and objectives as a means of allocating specific actions to sections of dramatic text. Ask students to complete the table, using Handout 37, explaining the concept of a rationale if necessary.

➢ Ask students to try Question 6, looking for ways of dividing up the second two phases into further phases.

➢ **Option**: Introduce a short evocative piece of music using either a digital music channel or favourite track on a CD. Aim to choose a track that might suit the opening of the play *Humble Boy*. Ask students to listen with their eyes closed. Introduce the concept of 'mood' and ask students to describe the mood of the music using a range of adjectives and adverbs. Ask them to note these words down in their Reflective Log as appropriate. Students can then be asked to reflect on the possible mood of the extract and particularly the mood of the beginning.

➢ Ask students to complete Question 7 on page 133 of the Student's Book, working on their own. Then read the sample student paragraph on page 133 and ask students to work on Questions 8 and 9, evaluating the success of the paragraph as a description of one of the 'touching moments' in the text.

➢ Ask students to work in pairs to develop ideas for dramatic staging for one of the key moments in the extract. Ask them to make notes under specific headings: lighting, set, performance, costume, etc. Share these ideas for staging and evaluate their possible dramatic impact.

➢ **Reflective Log**: Ask students to write a short summary paragraph identifying three key touching moments in the extract (number them) and analysing why an audience might find them touching.

APPLYING THE SKILLS (30–60 min)

Equipment: Student's Book, Reflective Log, copies of Scene 2 of *Humble Boy*

- As a group read Scene 2 from *Humble Boy*, a scene between Flora and her new boyfriend George. Discuss the contrast in dynamic between Flora and Felix and Flora and George. Divide Scene 2 into units and allocate a small unit to each small group of three or four students.

- Ask students to allocate objectives for the two characters for their specific section, reducing the text to no more than 10 words, which should be highlighted on the page. Ask them to explore the movement, gesture and posture of the characters, using just these few words.

  After a few minutes ask them to return to the full text and note the difference in dynamic and emphasis. Encourage them to experiment with pace, playing the scene at double speed and at half pace. Discuss the impact of these exercises on the development of character.

- **Reflective Log**: Ask students to reflect on the development of character using the following prompts: How did I develop the character? What was the impact on the audience? What could I do differently?

Give Extra Support: by working with students to develop frozen tableaux that clarify relationships, status and objectives. Support students in the highlighting of key words and discuss the impact of vocal emphasis by modelling different tones of voice.

Challenge: students to create a director's copy (annotated text) for Scene 2, marking decisions about proxemics, use of props and physicality.

CHECKING PROGRESS	Ask students to check their progress against the progress criteria on page 133 of the Student's Book and monitor their responses, making note of whether they have reached **Sound** or **Excellent** progress.

Unit 6.4 — Applying the skills – a learning sequence

| **SPOTLIGHT ON:** | How can I improve my responses to a longer script? |

This learning sequence is designed to accompany the activities in Unit 6.4 of the Student's Book, with a focus on the demands of both the practical and written examination. Teachers will be able to dip into and out of the activities, depending on the specific learning needs of the student group. Each section has been given an approximate time frame and, where a lesson is an average of an hour in length, we anticipate that the sequence might take up to three hours or three lessons.

KEY TERM:
archetype

Learning outcomes:
- **Respond to** and **explore** the opening to a longer script.
- **Understand** how performance, design or directorial decisions can impact on the interpretation of a dramatic script.

Differentiated learning outcomes:
- **All** students must focus on specific elements within a longer script and develop different skills to address them.
- **Most** students should be able to express their ideas for staging a text in written as well as practical formats.
- **Some** students could employ peer-assessment strategies to read and evaluate written responses to a longer script.

Resources:
- Student's Book: pp. 134–141
- Handout 14: Mind map
- Handout 32: Introduction to Stanislavski and 'The System'
- Handout 38: Introduction to 20th-century theatrical realism and Galsworthy
- Flipchart or a large piece paper and pens
- Coloured pens
- Reflective Log
- Photocopies of the extract on pages 134–137 of the Student's Book

Syllabus Assessment Objectives:

AO1: Understanding repertoire

Candidates will be assessed on their ability to demonstrate knowledge and understanding of the possibilities of repertoire, and how to interpret and realise it in a live performance.

AO3: Acting skills

Candidates will be assessed on their acting skills and their ability to communicate effectively to an audience.

Written work

Candidates' written answers should show practical and theoretical understanding of the play extract and devised piece they have performed as part of the course. They may need to write about a variety of aspects of:
- acting (e.g. interaction, pacing, physicality, proxemics, role, vocal expression)
- devising (e.g. characterisation, contrast, structure, tension)
- directing (e.g. advice to actors, directorial concept, mood, staging)
- design (costume and make-up, lighting, props, scenography, set, sound).

STARTING POINT (30–40 min)

Equipment: Reflective Log, Handout 32

- **Focus (20 min)**: This focus activity involves revision of the key features of Stanislavski's 'System', using Handout 32. Ask students to work in pairs to come up with a working definition of the terms: 'super-objective', 'through-line', 'unit' and 'objective'. Share the definitions and consolidate knowledge and understanding.

- **Warm-up (10–20 min)**: This activity is designed to help students to develop an understanding of the Stanislavskian imagination technique: 'Magic If'. Explain to students that you have lost your mobile phone. Describe the colour and shape, and explain that you can't call your own number because the phone is switched off. Ask students to engage in a thorough search for the phone, checking floor spaces, shelves, boxes, under furniture, etc. Run this for approximately two minutes and then announce that the phone has been found and was in your pocket all along.

  Next, ask students to re-run the search sequence 'as if' they did not know that the phone had been found and were still intent on finding it. Remind them to pay close attention to the 'truth' of their physical actions, facial expressions, language choices, etc. Use Handout 32 to explain Stanislavski's description of the evolution of the 'Magic If' as a tool for offering actors a psychological narrative to help to enrich the inner life of the character.

EXPLORING THE SKILLS (30–60 min) Equipment:

Student's Book, Handout 38

- Read the extract from John Galsworthy's play *Strife* on pages 134–137 of the Student's Book. Lead a discussion of the key features of the naturalistic genre and use Questions 1–3 on page 138 to explore key themes and ideas and mood and atmosphere.

- Introduce Handout 38 and give students a few minutes to read through it. Discuss with the students the key features of 20th-century social realism. Ask students to identify the features of the extract from *Strife* that would place the play within this genre – for example, 'working-class' dialogue concerning struggle and hardship; tension between characters from different social groups; the setting inside the home of a worker's family.

- **Option**: Ask students to focus on the character of Enid Underwood, daughter of the Chairman of the employing company. Use hot-seating to explore the psychological motivation for the character's visit to the Roberts' cottage. Lead the questioning by focusing on the prior relationship between Annie Roberts and Enid Underwood (Annie Roberts used to be Enid Underwood's maid, i.e. Annie was her servant).

- As a whole class, form a circle and ask one student to volunteer to play Enid and another Annie. Ask them to form a frozen tableau that demonstrates the relationship between the characters ten years before (when Enid was a girl). Once students are in position, ask others to mould them by gently manipulating the actors physically, like modelling clay. Reflect with the group on the impact of shifting proxemics, posture, gesture and facial expression. Repeat the exercise at two further points:
  - the scene between Enid and Annie at the beginning of the extract
  - the point immediately after Enid leaves the house (with Enid outside the cottage).

  Try introducing Mr Roberts and Mr Underwood to explore the impact of the presence of the men on the women.

DEVELOPING THE SKILLS (30–60 min)

Equipment: Student's Book

- Divide the students into pairs and allocate each pair one of the tasks and one of the exemplar student responses from pages 138–141 of the Student's Book. Ask the students to work through the questions and consider the strengths and areas for development in each student response.

- Ask students to write a paragraph that develops the answer. Weaker students might like to rewrite the current answer or continue the answer; stronger students should be encouraged to do both.

- **Option**: Ask students to write a short summary paragraph identifying three moments of tension in the extract (number them), describing ideas for staging (and characterisation) and analysing why they might be tense for an audience.

APPLYING THE SKILLS (30–60 min)

Equipment: Student's Book, Reflective Log, Handout 14, photocopies of the extract on pages 134–137

- With students working in small groups, refer them to the first section of the extract and ask them to divide the text into units and decide on super-objectives for the characters (drawing on the work carried out in Unit 6.3). Once the super-objectives are clear and defined by a verb – for example, 'to plead' – ask the students to rehearse the exchange between the characters by paying particular attention to movement, gesture, posture and facial expression.

- **Option**: Focus on the development of the characters of the women in the extract. Ask students to research the lives of women during the 19th-century industrial revolution in Britain, and to create a mind map (using Handout 14 if appropriate) that describes their lives. Ask students to pay particular attention to the differences that social class made to women's lives.

- As a final activity, ask the students to do Question 8 on page 141 of the Student's Book, concerning the development of the character of Enid and how her role helps to move the drama along.

- **Reflective Log**: Ask students to reflect on their responses to the long script, using the following prompts: How well did I understand the characters and the role they have in the extract? What supporting evidence was I able to identify? How well did I use appropriate dramatic terminology? What could I do differently?

Give Extra Support: by working with students to help them to develop their notes on characterisation. Remind them of key drama vocabulary that might be used to describe decisions an actor makes. Select two or three key moments in the extract to exemplify this approach and try modelling the writing.

Challenge: students to create a director's copy (annotated text) for the scene, marking decisions about proxemics, use of props and physicality.

CHECKING PROGRESS	Ask students to check their progress against the progress criteria on page 141 of the Student's Book and monitor their responses, making note of whether they have reached **Sound** or **Excellent** progress.

Handout 1: Brechtian devices

Device 1: Breaking the fourth wall

Brecht likes to make his audience fully aware that they are watching a play, not observing reality, so he has his actors speak directly to the audience. Then there is no illusion. The 'fourth wall' – the invisible wall between the actors and the audience – has been broken. The audience is no longer looking in on another world.

Device 2: Using a half curtain

To further alienate the audience and make them think rather than relax, Brecht uses a half curtain so that some of the workings of backstage are in full view (seeing actors changing costumes or swapping over props etc.). This serves to remind audiences that this is a play.

Device 3: Multi-role

Brecht uses multi-role (with an actor playing several roles in a play) so that the audience cannot get emotionally attached to a character. The audience should always be aware that an actor is playing a role. Another way to reinforce this is by letting several actors play the same part. A character might be signified through one piece of costume (such as a particular shawl or hat), or a distinctive prop (such as an umbrella or a rolled-up newspaper).

Device 4: Episodic structure

The play is split into episodes rather than acts and scenes. Each episode makes sense as a unit in its own right. The narrative can be non-linear – that is, not told in the chronological order of the events that took place.

Device 5: Use of song

To break up the action, Brecht uses song, much like a Greek chorus. He moves the action along by filling in the gaps in the story, comments on the actions of the characters, sets the scene in time and space, and adds comments on the themes.

Device 6: Social divide

Brecht drew attention to distinctions between social classes. For example, in *The Caucasian Chalk Circle*, Grusha the servant girl pretends to be of noble birth in order to protect Michael, the baby she is looking after. She is caught out when two ladies see the state of her hands while she is making a bed. They see that they are the hands of a girl who does housework. Small gestures such as these tell the audience a great deal about the class divide in society.

Device 7: Minimalist set and props

Brecht does not rely on a detailed set. Instead he uses a minimalist set with signifying props and items of costume – for example, a wooden spoon or a chef's hat for a chef.

Device 8: Making the audience think and act

Brecht wants to expose a division between the working class and the upper class: those who have to work hard to survive contrasted with those who own all the wealth (and have probably inherited it). He wants to make his audience think about the situation, recognise the injustice in it and react to it by doing something to improve the situation in real life.

Handout 2: Introduction to Greek theatre

Do some research and prepare a presentation on Greek theatre.

You could include the following:

- famous Greek playwrights and some of their plays (tragedy plays, comedy plays and satyr plays)
- the Greek chorus and their role in a play
- parts of the Greek theatre, such as:
    - skene
    - proskenium
    - paraskenia
    - parodos
    - kerkides
    - prohedria
    - diazoma
    - analemma
    - koilon / cavea / auditorium
- an image or illustration of a Greek theatre with your own labels added to it.

Remember: ancient Greek theatres were open-air, i.e. outside with no roof.

Handout 3: Flashcards – jobs, emotions, obstacles (1)

Jobs

HAIRDRESSER	BEAUTICIAN	ENGINEER
BANKER	NURSE	GRAPHIC ARTIST
TEACHER	DOCTOR	BUYER
SOLDIER	VET	FASHION DESIGNER
DETECTIVE	SOCIAL WORKER	SET DESIGNER
WINDOW CLEANER	RECEPTIONIST	LIGHTING DESIGNER
ACCOUNTANT	DENTIST	ELECTRICIAN
PILOT	AIR STEWARD	PLUMBER

Handout 3: Flashcards – jobs, emotions, obstacles (2)

Emotions

HAPPY	EXHAUSTED	FRUSTRATED
SAD	NERVOUS	IRRITATED
DEPRESSED	REFLECTIVE	FURIOUS
HYSTERICAL	HUNGRY	JEALOUS
CURIOUS	THIRSTY	ENVIOUS
ANXIOUS	FULL – EATEN TOO MUCH	BITTER
CONCERNED	ABSENT-MINDED	OVER-CONFIDENT
PHYSICALLY SICK	ANGRY	INSECURE

Collins Cambridge IGCSE™ Drama Teacher's Guide © HarperCollins *Publishers* 2016 — *Permission to photocopy*

Handout 3: Flashcards – jobs, emotions, obstacles (3)

Obstacles

A RAINY DAY	YOUR CHILDREN ARE ILL	FLOOD
SNOW	TOOTHACHE	LARGE HAILSTONES
ICE	LOST PURSE/WALLET	YOUR CLOTHES ARE NOT DRY
A LANDSLIDE OF MUD	LOST TRAVEL TICKET	LOST LAPTOP
NO TRAINS – LEAVES ON THE TRACK	LOST GLASSES	YOUR IDENTITY HAS BEEN STOLEN
CAR ACCIDENT – ROAD BLOCKED	FOG	PUNCTURE
POWER CUT – NO ELECTRICITY	HEATWAVE – ROADS ARE MELTING	ALARM DID NOT GO OFF
NO PHONE SIGNAL	GRANDMOTHER TAKEN TO HOSPITAL	EARTHQUAKE

Handout 4: Hot-seating example questions

When developing character, think about these headings:

- What the character does
- What the character says
- What other characters think of them
- What other characters say to them
- How other characters react to them

The method of hot-seating may be used for developing a role, or analysing a play post-performance. A character is questioned about their background, behaviour, motivation and objective.

Hot-seating is an excellent way of developing a character. Characters may be hot-seated individually, in pairs or small groups. It's best not to spend too much time focusing in on facts during hot-seating, but rather to concentrate on observations and personal feelings instead.

You might like to use some of these questions during hot-seating:

- Why did you say…?
- Why did you react that way?
- Why did you do…?
- How did it feel when… (something happened in the drama)?
- What is your deepest anxiety and fear and why?
- How did it feel when XY character… said/did… to/about you?
- How has your attitude changed towards…?
- What is your opinion of… and why?
- What did you mean when you said…?
- What would you do if…?
- What would you change about your character?
- What did you think about… (a person/situation/idea)?
- Who or what influences you?
- How would you describe yourself?

Handout 5: Vocal skills table

Volume	
Pitch	
Pace	
Direction	
Articulation	
Accent	
Tone	
Intonation	

Handout 6: Character profile

Name: **Age:**

Date of birth: **Place of birth:**

Education (e.g. qualifications, subjects):

Family background:

Social status:

Friends:

Lifestyle (e.g. music / sport / film / travel / cooking):

Height and weight:

Physical attributes (e.g. blue eyes, dark hair, muscly):

Gait (e.g. walks with back bent over / with hunched shoulders / with a limp / with head up):

Posture (e.g. bent over / straight back / head held high):

Gestures (e.g. uses hands while talking, points at people and things when in public, exaggerated waving):

Little habits (e.g. twiddles hair, bites nails, smooths skirt over knees when sitting):

Eye focus (e.g. eyes are fixed on a point ahead; the eyes wander):

Vocal delivery (e.g. fluency, pitch, volume, accent, intonation, use of pauses, speed):

Handout 7: Template for physicality

Posture	
Gait	
Funny little habits	
Facial expressions	
Eye focus	
Gestures	
Way of sitting	
Head movements	

Handout 8: List of character traits

List 1	List 2
kind	mean
happy	Sad
jolly	angry
approachable	temperamental
generous	selfish
sociable	self-centred
altruistic	lazy
selfless	unreliable
hardworking	always late
punctual	dishonest
reliable	malicious
reflective	impatient
trustworthy	jealous
humble	envious
intelligent	harsh
intellectual	severe
clever	strict
patient	unapproachable
even-tempered	foolish
well-educated	ignorant

Handout 9: Vocal expression (1)

Pace and tempo	
Inflection	
Modulation	
Stress	
Articulation	
Punctuation	
Syllable	
Vowel	
Consonant	
Pitch	

Handout 9: Vocal expression (2)

Enunciation/diction	
Onomatopoeic	
Intonation	
Accent	
Fluency	
Aside	
Projection	
Tone	
Iambic pentameter	
Vocal sounds	

Handout 10: Introduction to Shakespeare's language – the use of iambic pentameter (1)

Shakespeare's plays are written in verse and prose. Usually, the higher the social status of the character, the more likely they are to speak in verse. This is usually blank verse (that is, verse that does not rhyme), but sometimes a rhyming couplet will appear, generally at the end of a speech.

When faced with a Shakespearean speech, read it through a few times. Then annotate it using an edition that gives notes on each line. This will help you decipher the meaning. For example, look at the opening lines of *The Merchant of Venice*.

Extract:

ANTONIO

In sooth, I know not why I am so sad.	(1)
It wearies me, you say it wearies you;	(2)
But how I caught it, found it, or came by it,	(3)
What stuff 'tis made of, whereof it is born,	(4)
I am to learn;	(5)
And such a want-wit sadness makes of me	(6)
That I have much ado to know myself.	(7)

Explanations:

'In sooth' means *truly*. It is as if Antonio is answering a question that has just been put to him.

'I am to learn' means *I am yet to learn / to discover / find out*.

'want-wit' means *idiot* or *fool*. It could imply that he is absent-minded.

Interpretation:

Antonio is very miserable but does not know why.

Activities:

- Count the syllables in each line.
- How many syllables or beats are there in most of the lines?
- What is the effect of line 5 being so short, when you read the speech aloud?

    This line has only two feet (dimeter)

    Other patterns of feet:
    - monometer = one foot
    - trimeter = three feet
    - tetrameter = four feet
    - hexameter = six feet (an Alexandrine is a verse of six iambic feet, so sounds like Shakespeare's verse with one extra foot)
    - heptameter = seven feet

Handout 10: Introduction to Shakespeare's language – the use of iambic pentameter (2)

- How do you think Antonio feels at this point in the speech?
- In line 1, where would you place the stresses?
- Try to read it with the stress on the following words:

    Sooth, know, why, am, sad

    The line is broken up into five units:

    In sooth / I know / not why / I am / so sad.

    Each unit is called a foot, so there are five feet in this line. (pentameter)

    Each foot has two beats, so this makes 10 beats altogether.

    In each foot the stress is on the second syllable or beat, and this is called an iambic foot.

    Here, then, Shakespeare is using iambic pentameter.

- Does this work for the rest of the lines? Or does the pattern of stresses change anywhere?

    Try reading the speech, stressing the second syllable in each foot.

- In line 3, at the end, how do you read 'by it'? Could you make it sound like one word?
- Sometimes Shakespeare does play around with the pattern of stresses and uses some of the following devices:
    - Trochaic = stressed–unstressed (the opposite to iambic), e.g. 'never'
    - Anapestic = unstressed–unstressed–stressed, e.g. 'interrupt'
    - Dactylic = stressed–unstressed–unstressed, e.g. 'Washington'
    - Spondaic = stressed–stressed, e.g. 'heartbreak'
    - Pyrrhic = unstressed–unstressed, e.g. of the'

- For actors, it is useful to read the lines with the above knowledge as it helps them interpret the lines and give them meaning which is then projected to the audience. This helps the audience understand what the character is communicating. The stresses usually follow the patterns of natural speech, but there might be exceptions. Some English words are pronounced differently in different countries or by different speakers – for example, 'controversy' and 'contribute'. A good dictionary should show where the stressed and unstressed syllables should fall.

- Go back to the Caliban speech in Unit 2.3 page 25 and try to work out the meter of each line. How many syllables are there? How many feet? Is it iambic all the way through? What do the speech patterns tell you about the state of mind of the character? What is his social status?

- In the first line you can divide it into feet thus:

    All the / infect / ions that / the sun / sucks up?

- Which syllables are stressed? Mark them above the word with this mark: '

Handout 11: Ideas for preparing scripted work (1)

Duologue and dialogue extracts

- In pairs or groups, read the extract all the way through a couple of times. (If it is a complete play, a company would set aside enough time to read the whole play. Usually by this time the actors have been cast and they are then able to read their own parts during the read through. They read the play as if it were a performance; in other words, they do not stop to discuss the lines. They take a break between acts.)

- Check the meaning of any words or phrases you do not understand.

- Have an initial discussion about first reactions to the play or extract. Discuss the overall *meaning* and try to work out:
  - What is taking place and where it is taking place
  - When it is taking place (consider the historical era of the scene and what impact that might have)
  - Who is speaking and what their relationship is to the other characters
  - What we learn about each character
  - What each character's motivation is.

  Option: Carry out some research into the play:
  - When was the play written / set / first performed?
  - Read reviews by theatre critics about the play.
  - See whether the playwright has a website you can refer to.
  - See which theatre companies have performed the play and look at their website for extra resources or to see if there is any information about the set design, costumes or music.

- Break the scene down into small sections, or units, and start to examine the lines. Remember to look carefully for clues in the stage directions. Think about your own character and their status within the scene.
  - How are they feeling and why?
  - How do they react to what is said to them?
  - What tone of voice do you use to deliver the lines? This may change throughout the scene.

- Working on the extract in small sections, start to introduce gestures, where appropriate. Practise reading the lines first, and then stand up and introduce staging and movement. Work on the physicality of each character.

- Work out which words are stressed and decide how to say them with emphasis, but do not overdo it. Usually you are imitating natural speech patterns but delivering them with extra projection so that all of the audience can hear you. Depending on the age of the character, the lines may be delivered differently, perhaps more slowly for someone older or in authority, or to indicate someone who likes to be heard. A younger character may be excited and speak fast, desperate to get their words out before someone interrupts them. Match your delivery to the kind of character you are playing.

Handout 11: Ideas for preparing scripted work (2)

- For each section, annotate the script with notes of what has been discussed by the actors and the director. As you work with the other actors, relationships will build between the characters and you will become familiar with the lines. You will start to learn them, so the more you practise together, the better.

- When you know your lines, you will no longer need your script – what is called being 'off script'. You can now focus on physicality (particularly eye focus and hand gestures). Rehearse regularly so that you know the cues and the timing of the piece.

- Ask a friend or the director / your teacher to film it for you so that you can play it back and evaluate your performance.

- Do a technical rehearsal and, if using costumes, a dress rehearsal.

- Listen carefully to the feedback given by fellow students and your teacher/the director, and respond to it.

- **Option**: Try to watch the play on DVD, the internet or, better still, see a live performance of it. Write your own review of the performance.

Monologues

Follow the above process for a monologue, bearing in mind the following:

- You will have to learn any monologue working on your own, so set enough time aside to do this. Learn the lines in small sections, or chunks, and go through them on a daily basis so you do not forget them.

- Start by dividing the monologue into sections of two or three lines and work out the overall meaning. Learn a line at a time.

- Annotate the script and then work out how to deliver the lines according to emotions and character traits.

- Highlight key words so that you can remember the order of the sections.

- When preparing a monologue, you will be working more individually, but you can still work in pairs by taking it in turns to be an audience and a critic for each other. Take constructive feedback from peers and teachers as a form of help.

Handout 12: Ideas for exploring proxemics

1. A teenage son/daughter has just had an argument with one of his/her parents. In a tableau, show the child and parent and the distance between them. Which way does each one face? Use body language to show emotions such as anger.

2. Develop this by adding dialogue and continuing the argument where each character tries to have the last word. The argument could be about the bedroom being very untidy, coming home late or not answering the mobile phone when the parent calls.

3. Improvise the dialogue. Use natural gestures and body language. Does the distance between the characters increase or decrease? Is there much movement?

4. Decide how the argument ends. Does one character storm off, leaving the other angry and confused? Does either character win, or is this an unresolved argument that happens on a regular basis?

5. Run the scene again and introduce a third character who tries to persuade the other two characters to stop quarrelling. In a tableau show the distance between the original pair and the newcomer, who might be the other parent or a sibling. Think about gestures that could be used.

6. Using this new tableau, introduce dialogue. Improvise and see where the argument leads.

7. Is the argument resolved? Show the final tableau. Have the distances between characters become shorter? Are you now using close proxemics to show very familiar or even intimate relationships? Is the body language more relaxed?

8. Using the above method, try out other scenarios:
   - A prison guard restraining a dangerous prisoner who is trying to escape – More guards come to help. The prisoner breaks away and lets some of the prisoners out of their cells. There is a riot. Some prisoners go out on to the prison roof and are shouting and throwing bottles.
   - A pickpocket stealing a wallet or purse from someone – The thief runs off but is caught. There is a confrontation between the thief and the victim, with some passers-by trying to intervene to help calm the situation. A police officer arrives.
   - Two friends fishing from a riverbank – The hook of one fishing line catches on something heavy. The friends think it is an enormous fish and they work together to reel it in. They discover it is in fact a large bag with something very heavy inside.
   - The principal of a school discovering cheating – The principal goes back to his/her office after lessons have finished and all the pupils have left for the day and discovers two pupils are huddled together looking in a filing cabinet at exam papers.
   - A lifeguard at a swimming pool watching the pool – It is very crowded. Suddenly the lifeguard sees the body of what looks like a child floating just under the surface. He/She dives in to save the child. The parents come rushing over.

Handout 13: Vocal and physical warm-ups (1)

Breathing exercises

- Students stand comfortably in 'neutral' with feet parallel, legs slightly apart, and their arms by their sides and shoulders relaxed. Breathe in through the nose for four counts and out through the mouth for four counts. Repeat four times.

    Breathe in for two counts and on the breath out say *ah*. Repeat four times.

    Breathe in for four counts and on the breath out, say *ah*. Repeat four times.

- Breathe in, and on the breath out say the long vowel sounds *ay, ee, eye, oh, you*. Repeat three times. Breathe in for four counts and work through the short vowel sounds:
    - *The cat sat on the mat.*
    - *Fred met Ned who let Fred get wet.*
    - *Sid bit Lydia and Lydia hit Sid.*
    - *Not a lot of dots*
    - *Cut butter for fun*

- Practise the consonant sounds through repetition. Breathe for two counts or four counts and see how many repetitions of the pattern can be achieved before needing to breathe again:

    For example:

    p p p p p p p p …

    b b b b b b b b …

    t t t t t t t t t t …

    c c c c c c c c c c … as in *cut*

    Hiss hiss hiss hiss hiss

    then elongate the *ss* as in *hissssssss* while focusing on breathing out

- Then mix consonants.

    For example:

    ch ch ch ch ch ch ch

    sh sh sh sh sh sh sh sh

    th th th th th th th th

    st st st st st st st st st

- Next introduce longer words and ask students to pronounce all the letters clearly:

    repetitions   proxemics   dialogue   characterisation

- Say two words, leaving a slight space between them. Do not run the words together e.g. *performance space*. This should help students recognise the importance of diction.

Handout 13: Vocal and physical warm-ups (2)

Physical warm-ups

- Hamstring stretches on both legs for 10 counts each.
- Powerwalk around the space and swing the arms for 16 counts.
- Jog for 16 counts.
- Run and weave in and out of the group for 16 counts.
- Form a circle and gallop facing into the circle for eight counts.
- Change direction and gallop for eight counts.
- Repeat the galloping, facing out of the circle for eight counts in each direction.
- In pairs face each other and greet each other – handshakes, hugs, air kisses, high fives etc.

Handout 14: Mind map template

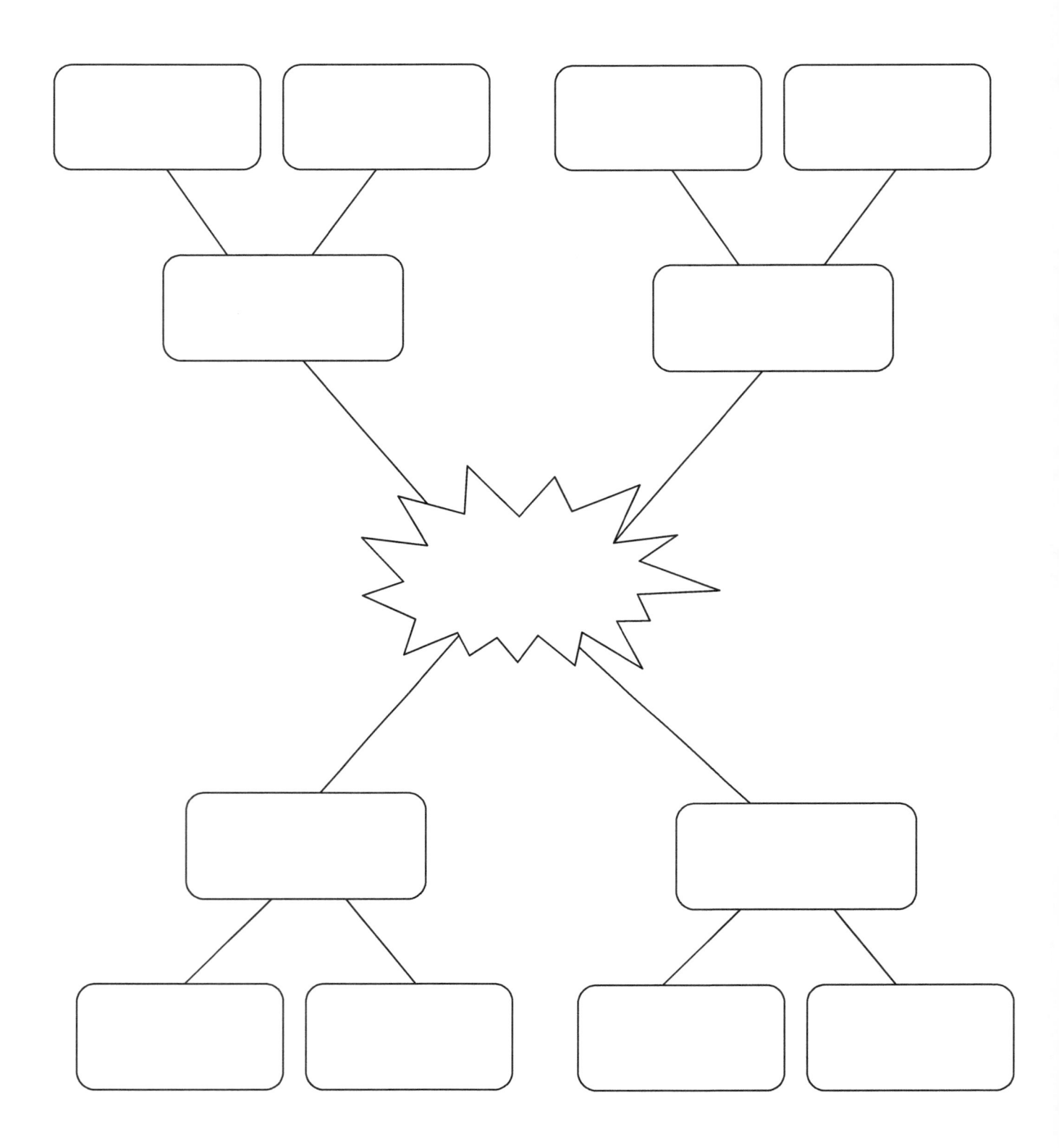

Handout 15: Lighting design table

Scene number and script cue	Type of lantern	Direction	Intensity	Colour	Special effects	Notes

Handout 16: Sound design table

Scenario	Atmospheric sound	Functional sound	Incidental sound
A busy garage			
A train station			
The beach in summer			
A busy restaurant			
A shopping mall			
A hairdressing salon			

Handout 17: Make-up design template (1)

Collins Cambridge IGCSE™ Drama Teacher's Guide © HarperCollins *Publishers* 2016 *Permission to photocopy*

Handout 17: Make-up design template (2)

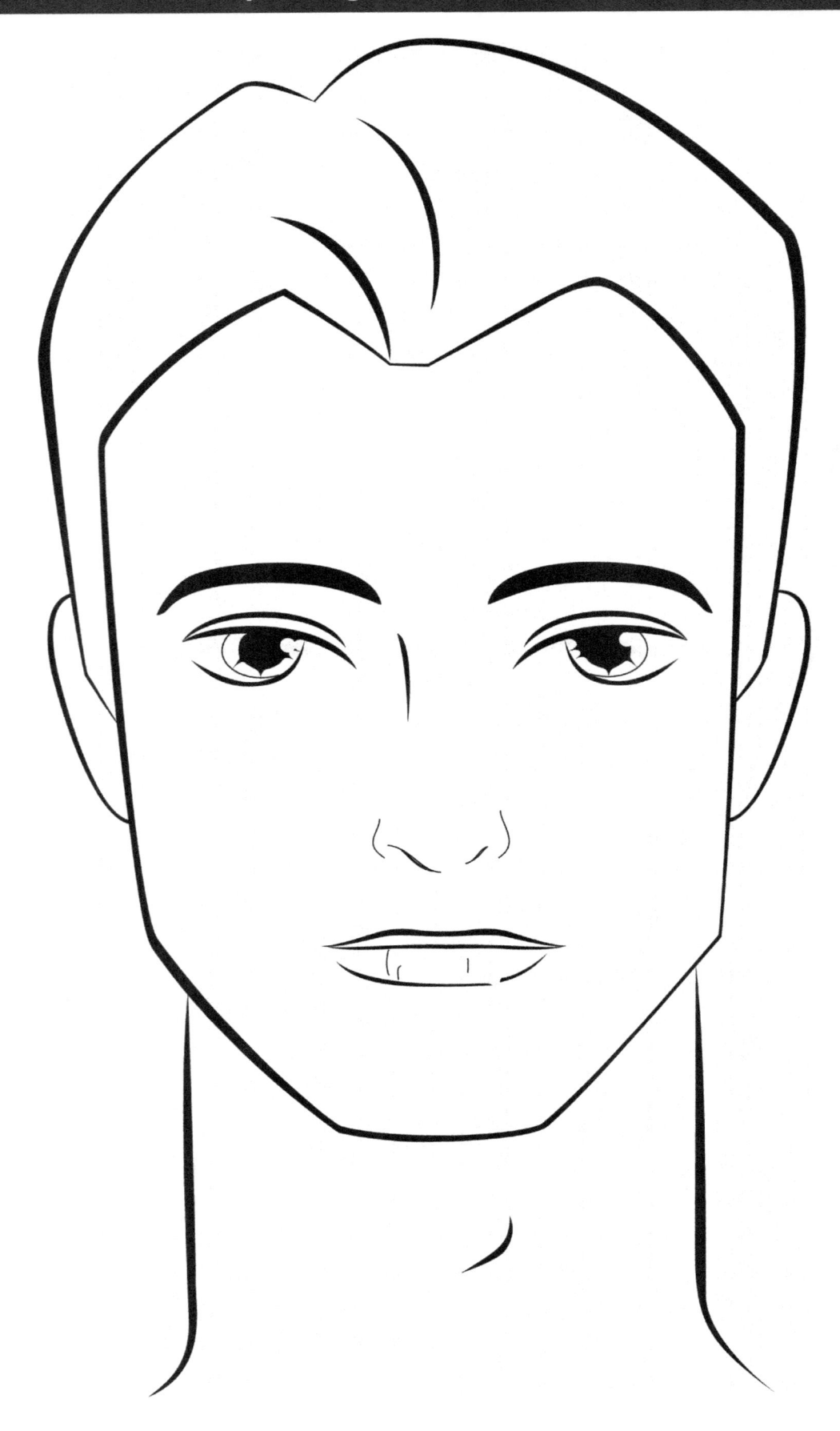

Collins Cambridge IGCSE™ Drama Teacher's Guide © HarperCollins Publishers 2016 *Permission to photocopy*

Handout 18: Plotting a typical *Commedia* storyline

Example 1: A young couple in love

Element	Description
1. Exposition	
2. Rising action	
3. Climax	
4. Falling action	
5. Resolution	

Handout 19: Stages of devised work

Stages of devised work	Mark between 1 (low) and 5 (high)	Reflective comment
1. Coming up with ideas (creativity)		
2. Structuring the drama (vision and strategy)		
3. Rehearsing and directing		
4. Performing (confidence and assertiveness)		
5. Reflecting and evaluating (thoughtfulness and attention to detail)		

Handout 20: Group roles

Note: Print, laminate, cut out each card, hole-punch and attach to safety pin or lanyard.

COORDINATOR

- Keep the group on task.
- Make sure everyone gets a fair turn.
- Get everyone to come to a decision.
- See the teacher or contact other groups if needed.
- Get involved! Talk, do and listen.

TROUBLESHOOTER

- Read instructions.
- Suggest ways of solving problems.
- Think of resources the group could use to solve problems.
- Get involved! Talk, do and listen.

GO-FOR

- Fetch objects and materials that the group needs to get the job done.
- Make sure resources are kept tidy and are put away.
- Get involved! Talk, do and listen.

RECORDER

- Write down the group's findings and decisions.
- Make sure the Reporter can read and understand the notes.
- Get involved! Talk, do and listen.

REPORTER

- Make sure you understand what the Recorder has written.
- Present what the group has done to the class or teacher.
- Be prepared to answer questions.
- Get involved! Talk, do and listen.

TIMEKEEPER

- Make sure the group is using time well.
- Tell the group when it is time to get going or move on.
- Tell the group when to finish and to pack up.
- Get involved! Talk, do and listen.

Collins Cambridge IGCSE™ Drama Teacher's Guide © HarperCollins Publishers 2016   Permission to photocopy

Handout 21: Character back story table

Element	Notes
Name of character (or nickname)	
Role	
Age	
Family (who, where, age, gender)	
Personality (friendly, aggressive, dreamy)	
Motive (what they want from the situation)	
A secret (something nobody else knows)	

Handout 22: Role on the wall

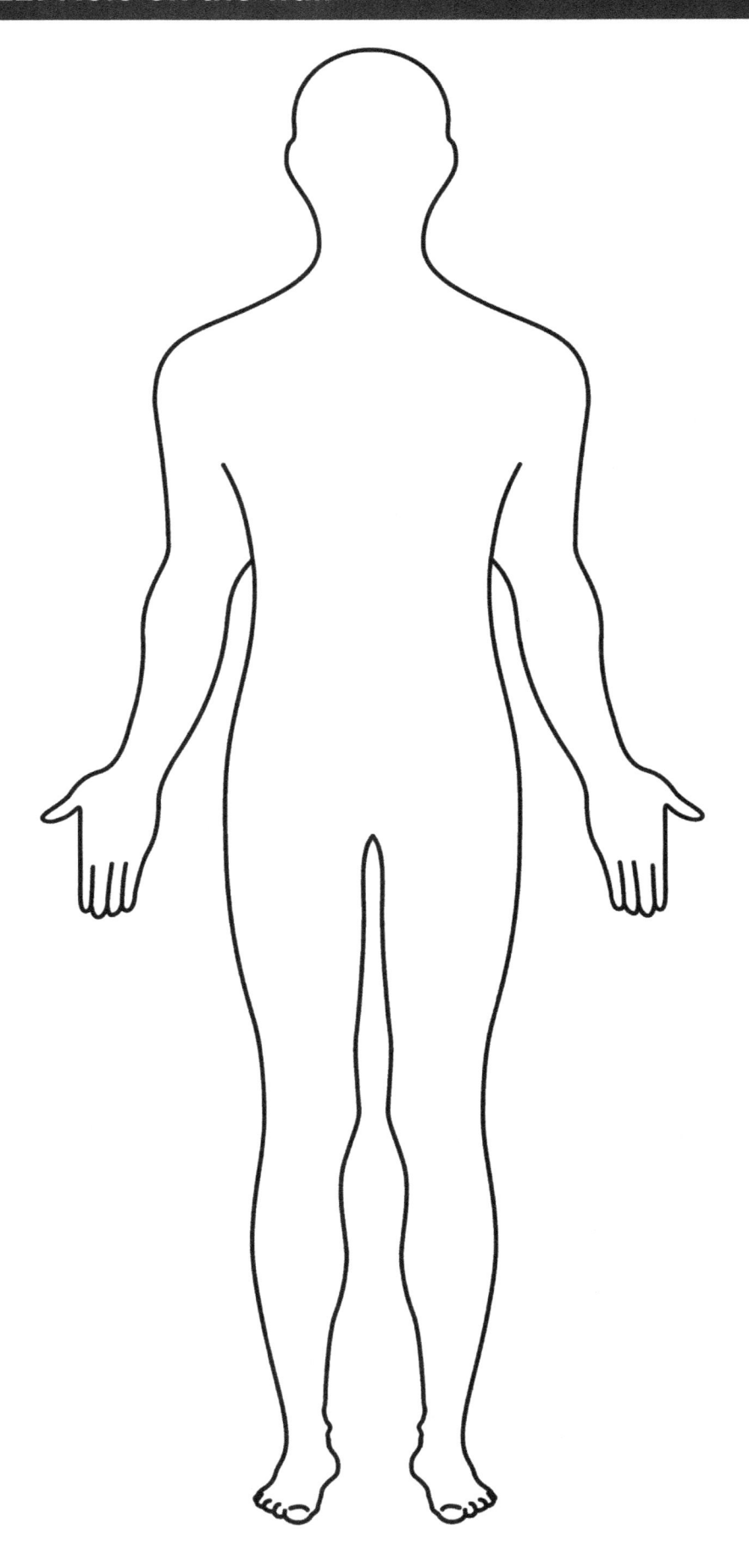

Handout 23: Different types of stage space (1)

When designing a stage, the actor–audience relationship must be carefully considered.

Amphitheatre

An amphitheatre is also known as an 'arena'.

Features:
- Large performance space.
- Audience in semi-circle with tiered seating.

History:
- Ancient Greek form of staging that started in the 5th century BC, and then also became the Roman model.

Fact:
- The biggest amphitheatre in the world is in Athens and seats 15,000 people, which is the same as a medium-sized football ground!

Advantages	Disadvantages
• Great for outdoors.	• Hard to create a bond between the audience because of the distance.
• Great for musicals / rock concerts.	• Outdoor staging relies heavily on weather.
• Great for large casts and 'epic' performances.	• Acoustics can cause difficulties.
• Great for large scenery, some lighting, sound and special effects.	• Can be lighting complications.
• Great for a football-crowd feel!	

Handout 23: Different types of stage space (2)

Thrust theatre

Features:
- A stage with the audience on three sides.

History:
- Derived from the Shakespearean era, during Elizabethan and Jacobean periods in England (1560–1625)

Facts:
- Historically, these theatres demonstrated the social and economic division in society. The galleries were where wealthy people sat, showing their high status, while the stalls (lower down and more uncomfortable) were where the poorer viewers sat or stood.

Advantages	Disadvantages
• Great for large-scale productions. • More intimate, as actors are closer to the audience and surrounded by them. • Large items of set can be used upstage without interfering with sightlines. • Most plays work well in this staging.	• Props / furniture cause sightline problems. • 'Blocking' needs to be precise (i.e. direction given to actors as to where they should stand or move to during the course of the play. Actors are given these bits of direction during blocking rehearsals); 'spiking' is essential during the technical rehearsal (i.e. putting tape or sometimes paint markings on the stage to indicate where props, furniture, and sometimes actors, will be placed). • Props plot is also essential. • Actors have to interact with all three sides of audience. • Lighting plot needs to be more complex. • Entrances / exits / wings need to be thought out because of sightlines. • The stage floor is a vital part of the set design because of the audience seating. • Scene changes have to be done in front of the audience.

Handout 23: Different types of stage space (3)

Proscenium arch

Features:
- An arch is built to accommodate the curtain.
- It creates a 'picture frame' effect for the audience, with a single view as when watching television.
- The audience or stage is always raked.

History:
- From the late 17th century until the early 20th century this was the standard form of staging for most theatres in Britain.

Facts:
- Traditionally, the curtain was always dropped for scene changes, but it rarely is in modern theatre today.
- In the West End, in London, and other older regional theatres, the theatres retain their 'dividing line' (fourth wall).

Advantages	Disadvantages
• Audiences are comfortable, as this is the most familiar staging.	• Difficult for an audience to become heavily involved.
• The presence of the 'fourth wall' between stage and audience creates a sense of 'us and them', as if the audience are spying on the real lives of characters. Realistic sets are easy to create.	• Blocking needs to be natural, while also ensuring that the audience can see everything that is going on.
• The fourth wall can be broken deliberately to break the illusion of reality.	• Blocking needs to ensure actors' positioning isn't too linear in the performance and no one has their back to the audience (which makes it hard for the audience to hear).
• Blocking is easier with entrances and exits.	• Furniture needs to be placed with the audience in mind – good prop plot and spike during technical rehearsal.
• Technical effects are easier to achieve.	
• Most types and scales of performance can be successful.	

Handout 23: Different types of stage space (4)

In-the-round

Features:
- 'In-the-round' means that the audience surrounds the stage.
- The performing area doesn't necessarily need to be round, but the audience is positioned on all sides of the performers.
- The stage is at floor level with a raked audience all the way around – similar to an amphitheatre, but the sides are not semi-circular.

Facts:
- Few theatres have main houses that are designed for in-the-round performances – but some can adapt.
- Most studio theatres are designed to be able to adapt to an in-the-round performance.

Advantages	Disadvantages
• The audience–actor bond is strong and intimate because the actors are close to the audience.	• Similar to thrust issues but even more so!
• It is impossible to have a realistic set in-the-round – this enhances imagination of those watching.	• Unless you can raise the audience you will struggle with sightline problems.
• The audience has to create a sense of environment themselves.	• Realism can't be used with this set.
• Enables a more naturalistic performance, as actors will have their backs to someone at some stage.	• Greater restrictions for designers of set, lighting and sound.
• Scene changes can happen as part of the performance – by cast or stage management in costume.	• Restrictions on the placing of furniture and focus of lights.
	• Blocking has to be highly accurate because of performing to four sides.
	• Actors can be subtle because they have an audience all around.

Handout 23: Different types of stage space (5)

Traverse stage

Features:
- Also so known as 'theatre in the corridor', it is a corridor between two blocks of audience.

Facts:
- This is a very uncommon type of stage form.
- Few theatres are built to accommodate this exclusively.
- The Traverse Theatre in Edinburgh, Scotland, has retained its name, but now has a new building and stages in other forms.

Advantages	Disadvantages
• Audience has to use imagination because of set restrictions (as with in-the-round).	• Suitable only for a relatively small audience, although there are exceptions.
• Doors and walls can be used to create a corridor feel without interfering with sightlines.	• Audience ideally needs to be raked in tiers like a catwalk, which can be hard to create.
• Simple form to create in a studio theatre.	• Using each extreme end of the stage can create problems for audience sightlines and can cause a 'Wimbledon effect' (repeatedly having to turn your head from side to side) for the audience, which can be uncomfortable.
• Good staging option for small audiences.	
• Good for enabling use of movement, allowing swift changes of location in a fast-paced play.	• During scene changes, blocking usually means one set of actors has to exit one end and the new cast / new scene comes on from the other end.
	• Scene changes have to be carried out in full view of the audience. (**Note**: this could be seen as an advantage if the play is taking a Brechtian approach).

Handout 23: Different types of stage space (6)

Promenade theatre

Features:
- Audience and performers occupy the same space.
- The audience follows the performers from one area to the next.
- Usually no seating.

History:
- This is a rare form of theatre that has developed in the last 20 years.

Facts:
- Usually performed in large spaces, although 'fringe' theatres use this effectively.

Advantages	Disadvantages
- Usually staged simply and cheaply. - Exciting form of staging that has a real sense of community. - The audience are usually incorporated into the performance. - Lighting can be used to point to where action is moving to.	- Difficult to rehearse with so much audience participation. - Audience may be hard to control – may have to have an invited audience to rehearsals. - Lighting is complex because of the risk of glare into the audience. - Sound design is difficult – placing of speakers needs a lot of thought. - There are health and safety issues such as trailing cables and trip hazards. - Shorter members of the audience have to be thought of, as they are disadvantaged. - Disabled audience members must be considered.

Handout 23: Different types of stage space (7)

Non-conventional theatre

Have you heard of, or have you maybe seen, any non-conventional theatre?

Features:
- Locations that can be used include:
  - car parks
  - closed-off streets
  - restaurants.

History:
- Created in the late 20th / 21st century.

Facts:
- Interest has increased since the growth of the Edinburgh Fringe Festival in Scotland.

Advantages	Disadvantages
• Unusual and exciting.	• Public might not appreciate that it is a performance in public.
• Unique theatre – no two performances will be the same.	• Technical challenges.
• Very site specific.	• Limited audiences.
• Very imaginative.	• Problems with costume changes, entrances and exits.

Look around your school. Can you identify areas where non-conventional theatre could take place?

Handout 24: Drawing ground plans (1)

What is a ground plan?

A 'ground plan' is a bird's-eye view of a set, drawn using symbols for both staging and design.

A 'bird's-eye view' means a view from above.

A ground plan must have…

- **K** a **K**ey
- **A** **A**udience and **A**rrows
- **V** **V**iability – it has to work
- **E** **E**ntrances and **E**xits
- **S** **S**ymbols, **S**cale and **S**taging

Drawing your own ground plans

➢ Start by drawing the basic outline of your stage and add in where the audience is positioned in relation to the stage.

➢ Add arrows to show the direction in which the audience is looking.

➢ The six types of stage are shown on the following pages.

Handout 24: Drawing ground plans (2)

End-on

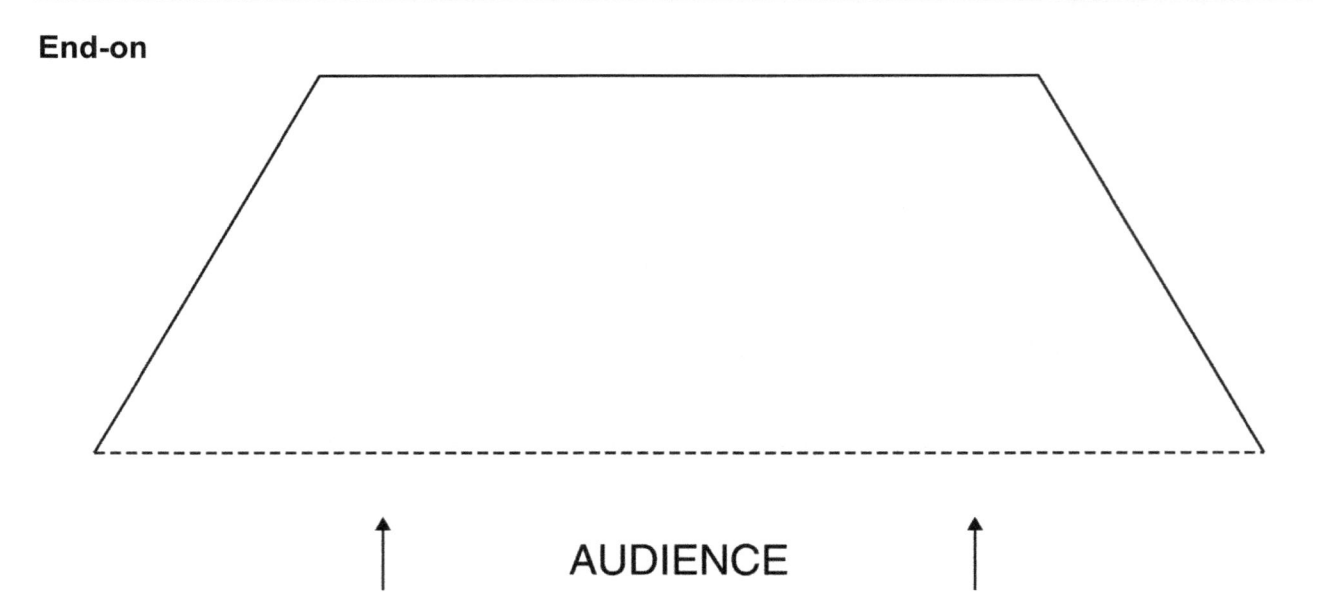

↑ AUDIENCE ↑

Traverse

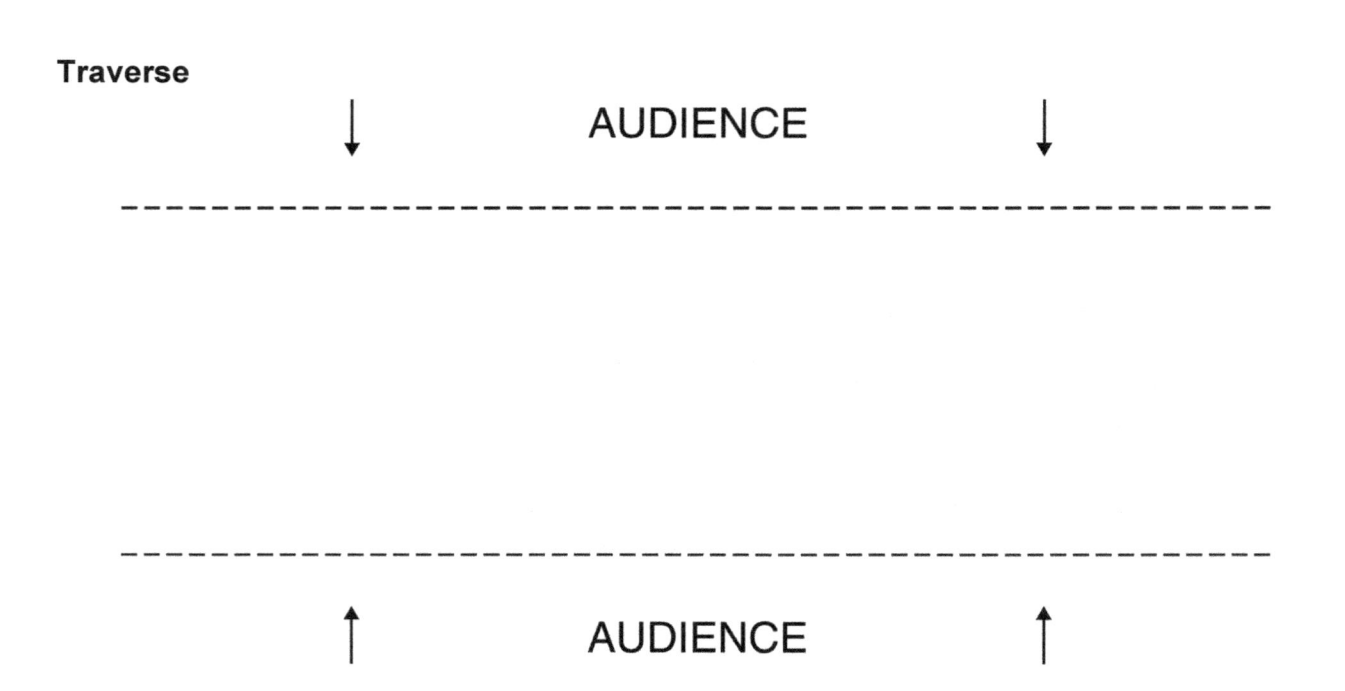

↓ AUDIENCE ↓

↑ AUDIENCE ↑

Handout 24: Drawing ground plans (3)

Thrust

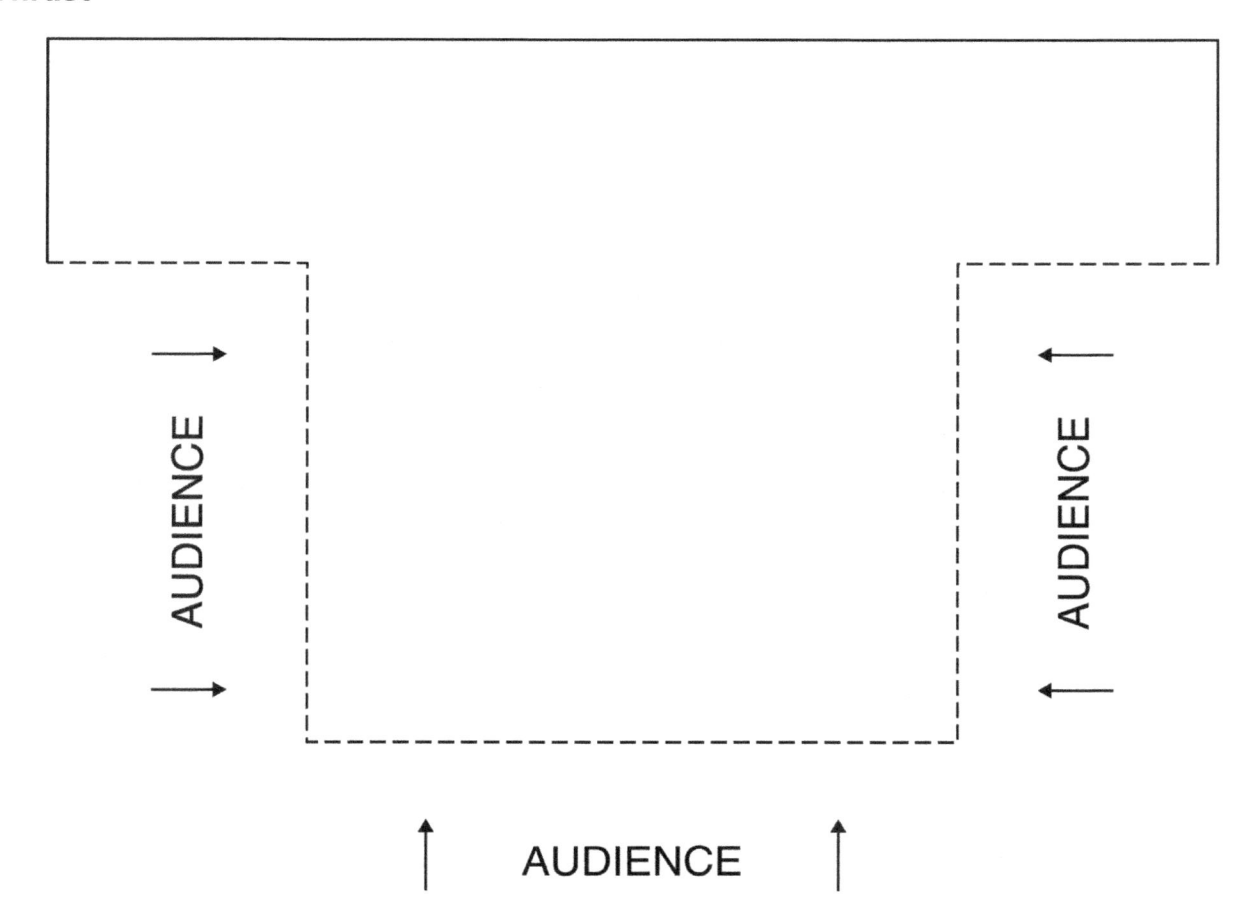

[Ground plan diagram showing a thrust stage: a rectangular stage area at the top with a smaller rectangular thrust extending downward. AUDIENCE is labelled on the left side (with arrows pointing right toward the stage), on the right side (with arrows pointing left toward the stage), and at the bottom (with arrows pointing up toward the stage).]

Handout 24: Drawing ground plans (4)

In-the-round

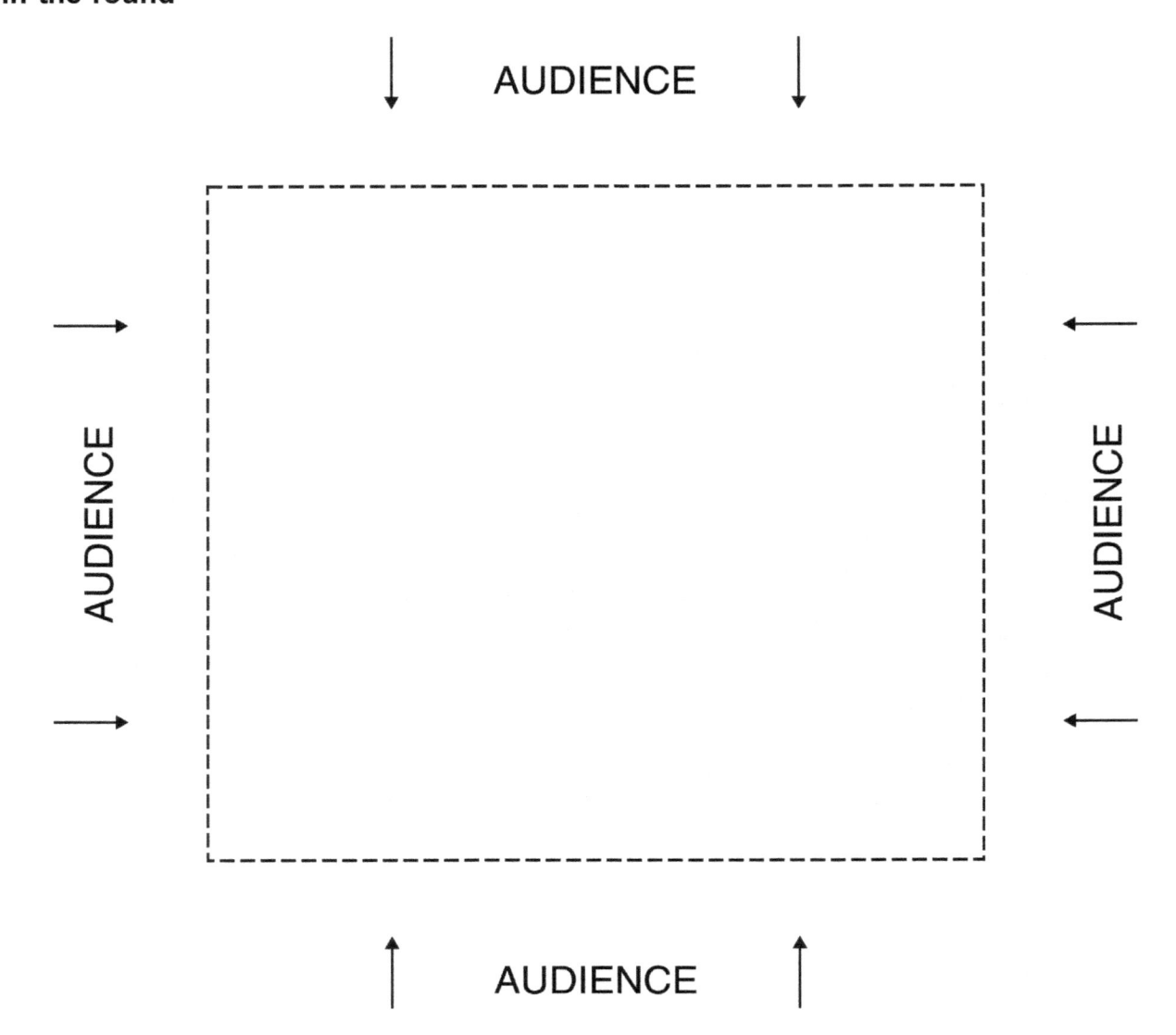

AUDIENCE

AUDIENCE

AUDIENCE

AUDIENCE

Handout 24: Drawing ground plans (5)

Proscenium arch

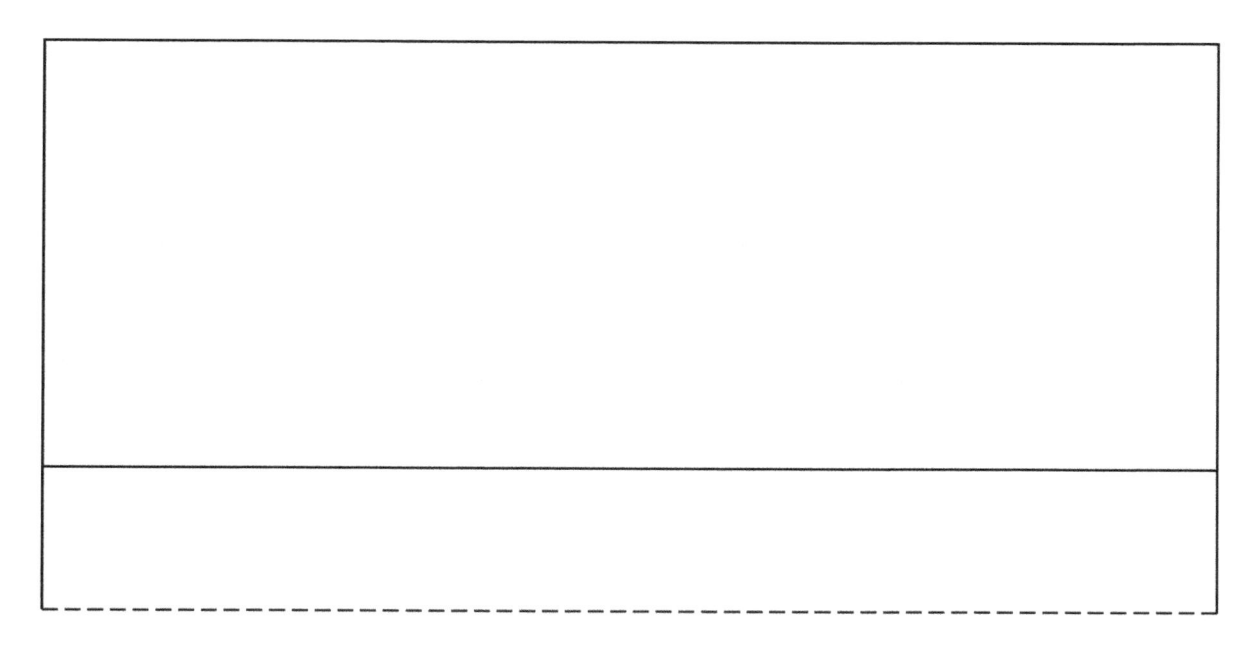

AUDIENCE

Promenade

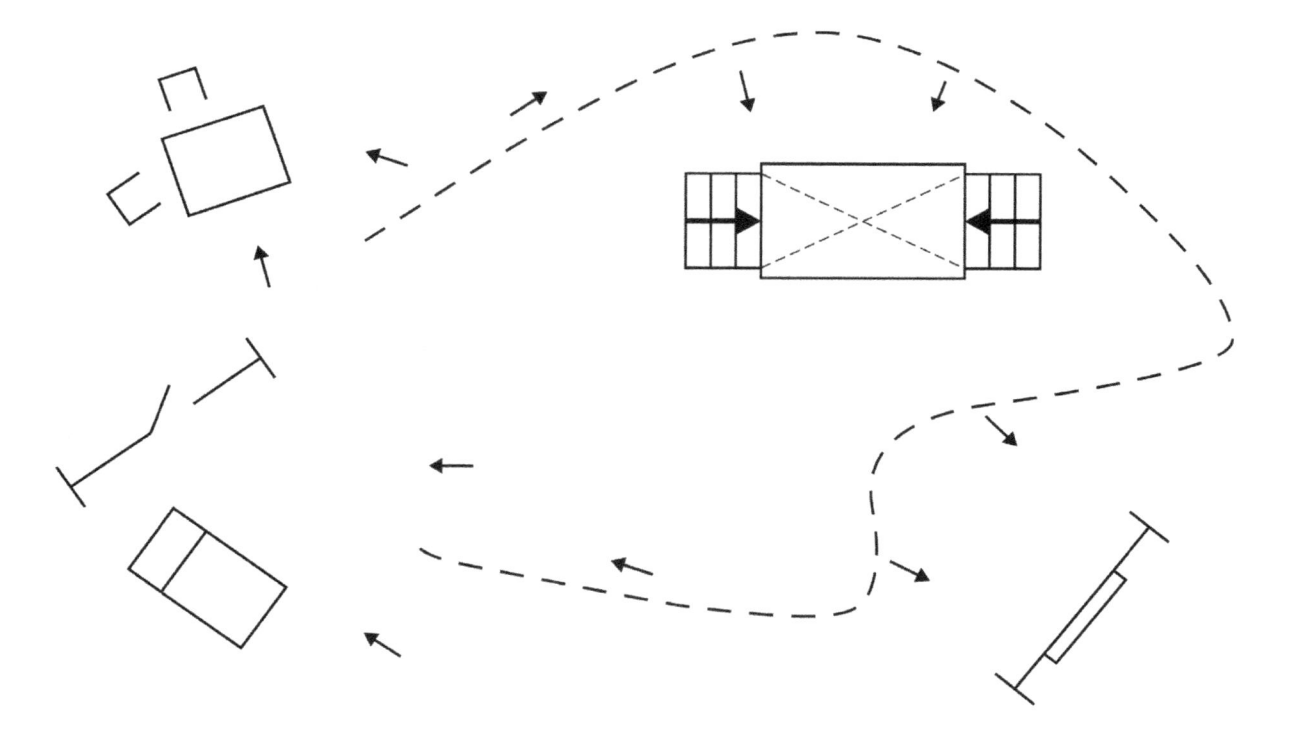

Collins Cambridge IGCSE™ Drama Teacher's Guide © HarperCollins *Publishers* 2016   *Permission to photocopy*

Handout 24: Drawing ground plans (6)

Symbols

The following pages demonstrate the standard symbols that should be used when drawing ground plans.

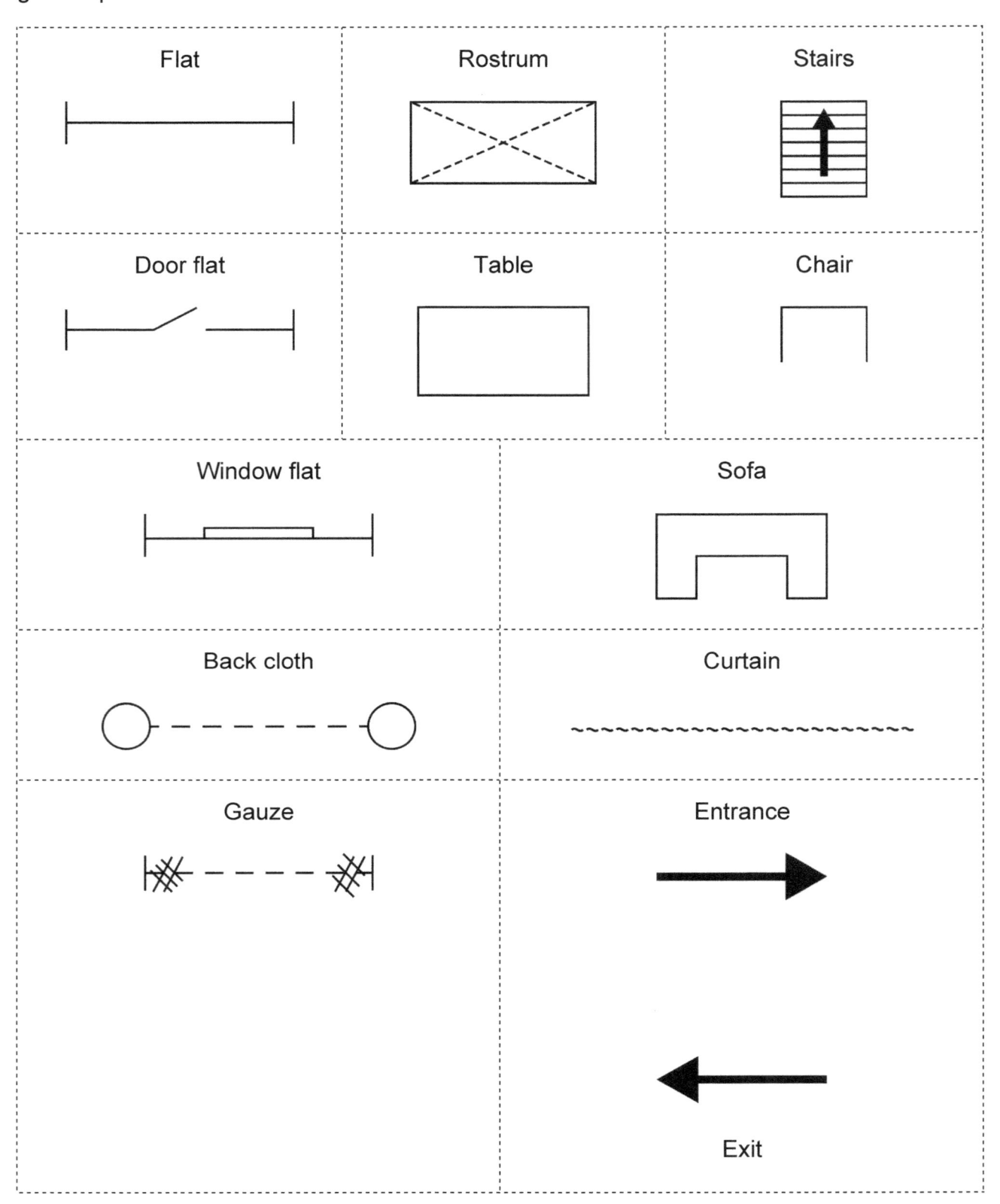

Flat	Rostrum	Stairs
Door flat	Table	Chair
Window flat	Sofa	
Back cloth	Curtain	
Gauze	Entrance	
	Exit	

Collins Cambridge IGCSE™ Drama Teacher's Guide © HarperCollins *Publishers* 2016   *Permission to photocopy*

Handout 24: Drawing ground plans (7)

This set has to work! Look at it. Is it viable?

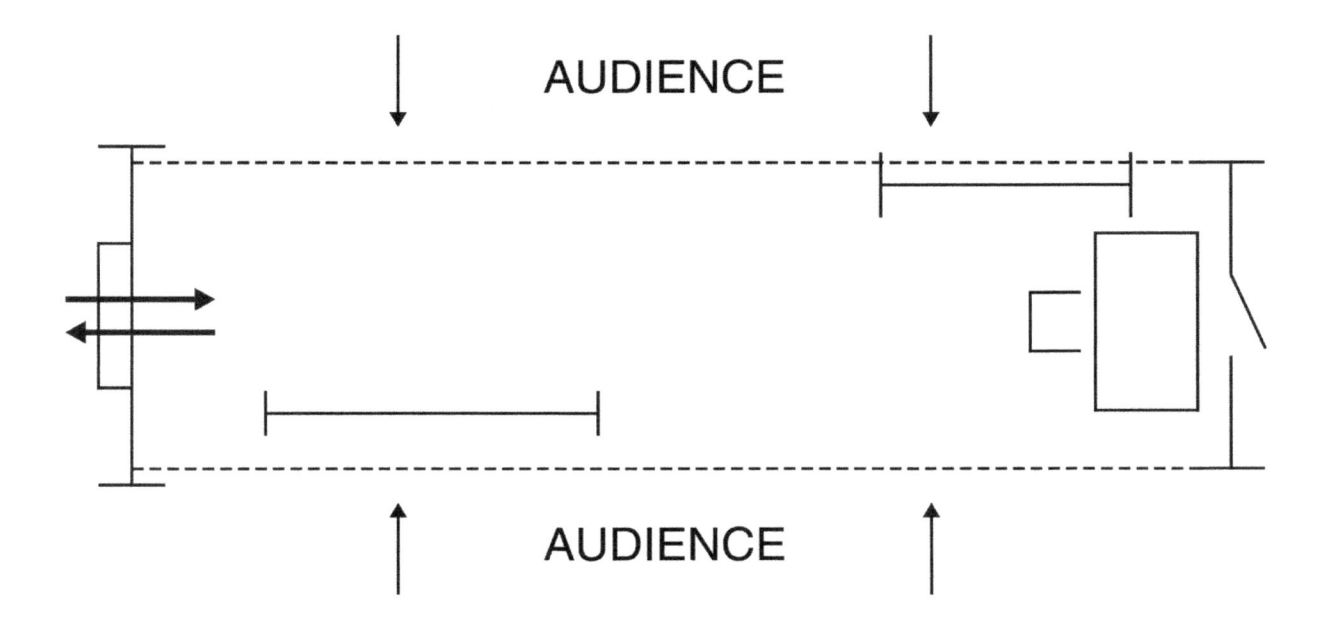

Answer: It is not viable!

There are a number of problems with this set in terms of viability … what are they? Redraw it below, so that it is viable.

Handout 24: Drawing ground plans (8)

The key

The key explains all the symbols on the ground plan and is drawn alongside or below it:

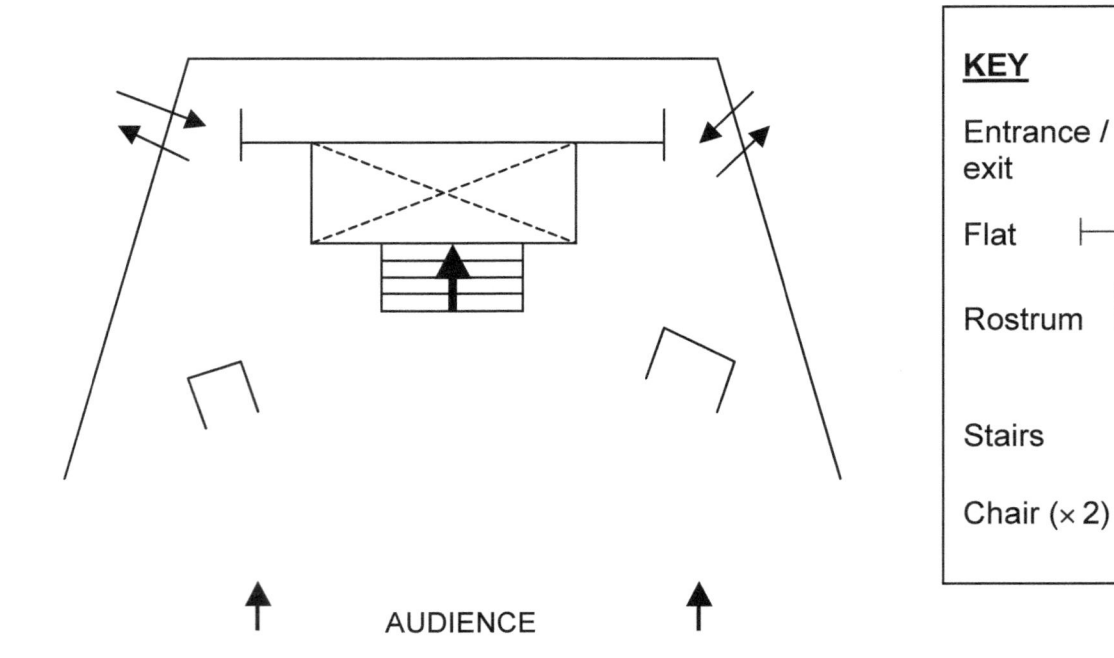

KEY	
Entrance / exit	→ ←
Flat	⊢——⊣
Rostrum	▨
Stairs	▦↑
Chair (× 2)	☐

AUDIENCE

New symbols

- If you have a piece of set, which requires you to create a new symbol, keep it simple – and remember to mark it in your key.
- Two examples are shown below:

Car

Fireplace

Scale

- Symbols should be drawn with some consideration of scale.
- For instance:
    - A kitchen table is four or six times larger than the size of a chair.
    - A chair is usually a third of the size of a sofa.
    - Flats are not smaller than chairs.
    - Tables are not bigger than flats.
    - Doors are not larger than chairs.

Collins Cambridge IGCSE™ Drama Teacher's Guide © HarperCollins *Publishers* 2016   Permission to photocopy

Handout 24: Drawing ground plans (9)

Not to scale!

What is wrong with the following plan?

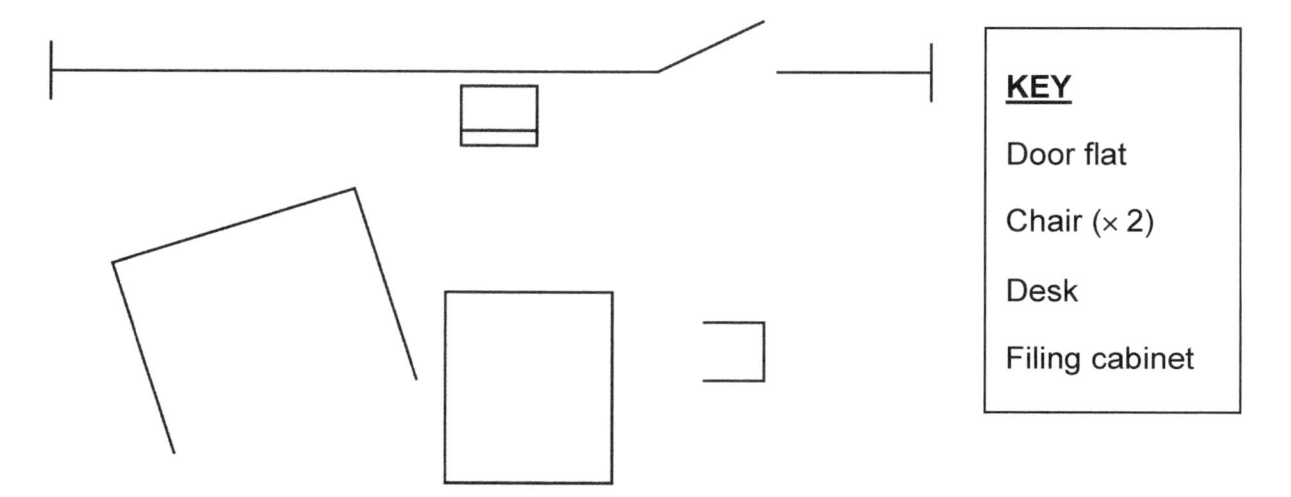

KEY

Door flat

Chair (× 2)

Desk

Filing cabinet

Hints for drawing ground plans:
- It is a good idea to use a pencil, not a pen.
- Always have an eraser and a ruler handy.
- Remember KAVES – keep it neat and simple.
- Never put props on a ground plan.

Now try drawing the following ground plans:

- An office with a desk, two chairs, a filing cabinet, a door flat, a window flat and a flat. The set is on an end-on stage.
- A bedroom with a door flat, a desk, a chair, a bed and a bedside table. The set is on a thrust stage.
- A police interview room with a table, three chairs, a door flat and a flat with two-way mirror attached. The set is on a traverse stage.
- A bar with two tables and four stools, a jukebox, a men's washroom with one stall and a urinal, and an area outside with chairs and a heater. The set is on a promenade stage.

Collins Cambridge IGCSE™ Drama Teacher's Guide © HarperCollins Publishers 2016   *Permission to photocopy*

Handout 25: Timeline flashcards

(cut along lines and laminate)

Before

During

After

Collins Cambridge IGCSE™ Drama Teacher's Guide © HarperCollins *Publishers* 2016   *Permission to photocopy*

Handout 26: Extract from *Maria Marten – The Murder in the Red Barn* (1)

Maria Marten – The Murder in the Red Barn
Adaptation of the traditional melodrama, by Christopher Denys

Background:

Melodrama was a dramatic form that thrived and grew in British theatre from the 1600s into the 1950s. *Maria Marten – the Murder in the Red Barn* was one of the key pieces of this form. Melodrama frequently has outrageous plots and special effects, and yet has reality to it. *Maria Marten* is certainly based on reality, because Maria Marten and William Corder were real people and in its time the murder caused an outrage and a sensation. William Corder murdered Maria Marten in 1827, and buried her body in the Red Barn, in Polestead, Suffolk, in England. As soon as the crime was discovered, portable theatres were thrilling and shocking audiences in barns and fairgrounds all over England with their individual versions of the story.

Scene 14: INSIDE THE RED BARN

CORDER stands by the freshly dug grave. He leans the spade against the wall and mops his brow.

CORDER: All is complete. I now await my victim. Will she come? Oh yes. A woman is fool enough to do anything for the man she loves. Hark, 'tis her footstep!

She comes in good heart, with hope and good cheer.
Little does she know that death is so near. *(He draws back)*

Enter MARIA, fearfully, at the door R.

MARIA: William? Not here. Where can he be? What ails me? A weight is at my heart as if it told some evil. And this old barn – how like a vault it looks. Fear steals upon me. I tremble in every limb. I will return to my home at once.

CORDER: *(Stepping forward)* Stay, Maria!

MARIA: Oh, William. I am so glad you are here. You don't know how frightened I have been.

CORDER: Did any one see you cross the fields?

MARIA: Not a soul – I remembered your instructions.

CORDER: That's good. Now, Maria, do you remember a few days ago threatening to betray me about the child to Constable Ayers?

MARIA: A girlish threat made in the heat of temper, because you refused to do justice to one you had wronged so greatly. Do not speak of that now. Let us leave this place.

CORDER: *(Gripping her wrist)* Not yet, Maria. Do you think my life is to be held at the mercy of a silly girl? *(Dragging her to the grave)* No. Look what I have made here.

MARIA: A pit? A trench? Ah! A grave! Oh, William, what means this?

CORDER: You are a clog upon my actions, Maria – a chain that keeps me from reaching my ambition's height. *(Drawing a knife)* So you must die.

Handout 26: Extract from *Maria Marten – The Murder in the Red Barn* (2)

MARIA: But nay, not by your hand! Not by the hand that I have clasped in love and faithfulness. Oh! Pity, William. What do you mean to do?

Music. Act One Finale. (Trio from 'FAUST' by C. Gounod.)

CORDER: To kill you!
Destroy you!
And to bury you here.
(seizing her) No, you shall not take flight!
For you must die tonight!

MARIA: This my grave?
Sure, you rave!
You are ill, will you betray me?
And with cold heart seek now to slay me?
I am your wife!
Your words cut me like a knife! *(She twists the knife from his hand)*

CORDER: You must die – I command *(Seizing her by the throat)*

MARIA: *(Struggling)* But why? Stay your hand!

CORDER: I'll no longer stay. You must die ere the day,
For I fear you'll betray.
So – no delay.
Tis time now to kneel and pray!

MARIA: Ah, nay,
my love, recall
I say –
Love conquers all!

She struggles and breaks free, imploring mercy.

I who love thee more than my life,
have ever been thy faithful wife.
By heaven, set in glory above me,
I swear that I will always love thee.
I who love thee more than my life
will ever be thy faithful wife.

CORDER: *(Drawing his pistol)* Cease now your tears,
you must die!

MARIA: I who love thee more than my life
will ever be thy faithful wife.

CORDER: *(Shoots her)* Death is nigh!

MARIA: *(Falling)* O, save me – ere I perish for ever!

CORDER: I am safe now!

Handout 26: Extract from *Maria Marten – The Murder in the Red Barn* (3)

MARIA: O, save me – ere I perish for ever!

CORDER: Time to take flight
into the night

MARIA: May blessed angels bear my soul to heaven.

Clouds fly in and slide on. ANGELS appear resplendent in Heaven above R. and L. with the Ghost of ZELLA LEE.

CORDER: And the day dawns

MARIA: *(Appealing to the Angels)* Holy angels, in heaven blessed –

CORDER: I must race
from this place
ere I suffer disgrace.

MARIA: *(Sinking into the grave)* My spirit longs, with thee, to rest!

CORDER: Before the dawn, I must haste away.

MARIA & ANGELS: O pardon, heaven grant I/she implore/s thee

CORDER: No remorse!
Swiftly to horse!

MARIA & ANGELS: For soon I/she shall appear before thee!

MARIA disappears into the grave.

CORDER: First take a moment to cover the grave well.

MARIA & ANGELS: Holy angels, in heaven blest.

MARIA's soul (gauze – or a projection onto a smoke curtain) flies gracefully out of the grave and slowly up to Heaven during:

MARIA & ANGELS: My/Her spirit longs with thee to rest.

CORDER: *(Turning, seeing the ANGELS and MARIA's soul)* Curse my eyes!
Does she arise?
Shall she find paradise?
Ah then my soul shall be damned – to hell!

He collapses D.L. as MARIA's soul is received by the ANGELS.

Curtain Music

CURTAIN – END OF PART ONE.

Handout 27: Introduction to Victorian melodrama (1)

The Industrial Revolution
- 19th-century advances in science and technology
- shift from rural to urban living
- scientific discoveries led to fundamental change to commerce
- increasing urban divide between rich and poor
- child labour

Living conditions and consequences
- terrible urban overcrowding
- disease – especially as a result of poor sanitary conditions
- alcoholism
- role of church in alleviating poverty

What does *melodrama* mean?
- A drama characterised by exaggerated emotions, stereotypical characters, and interpersonal conflicts.
    - *Melo* = 'Music'
    - *Drama* = 'Drama'
- Theatres were required to have musical intervals.
- Popular romantic dramas known as Melo-dramas.
- Included songs during the performances and between scenes and at interval.
- Romanticism developing in theatre – characterised by sweeping gestures and elaborate sets.

History of melodrama
- Became a theatrical form in about 1800
- René Charles Guilbert de Pixerécourt
    - *La femme à deux maris*
- First English play to be called a Melodrama
    - *A Tale of Mystery* (1802) by Thomas Holcroft
- Reaction to immorality of English restoration plays (of the 18th century)

Characteristics
- Fast-paced dramatic plots: exciting story, suspense, plot twists (discoveries, hairbreadth escapes, secret passages, hiding places, disguises)
- Audience response: very basic emotional appeals involve 'arousal of pity and indignation at the wrongful oppression of good people, and intense dislike for wicked oppressors'
- Exotic locations: exotic/far away or ugly/desperate or lush/beautiful – never ordinary

Handout 27: Introduction to Victorian melodrama (2)

Melodrama's stock characters
- **Hero**: handsome, strong, brave, honest and reliable.
  - Status: middle class or higher
- **Heroine**: Beautiful, courageous, innocent and vulnerable.
  - Status: middle class or higher
- **Villain**: Cunning, without morals, dishonest, cruel and evil.
  - Status: middle class or higher
- **Villain's accomplice**: Comic relief, bumbling sidekick.
  - Status: lower class
- **Faithful servant**: Also provides comic relief, does dirty work. Usually discovers evidence against the villain.
  - Status: lower class
- **Maid servant**: Female character who is lively and flirts with the faithful servant.
  - Status: lower class

Staging and technology
- Proscenium arch
- Machinery available for complicated sets
  - fly towers and counterweight
  - treadmills
  - electric lighting
- 'Sensation' melodramas
  - disasters happened on stage
  - *The Poor of New York* – Dion Boucicault (Real fire engines put out a real fire)

Popular Victorian Melodramas
- *Maria Marten or The Murder in the Red Barn*, Andrew Melville (1919)
- *A Tale of Mystery*, Thomas Holcroft (1802)
- *The Streets of London*, Dion Boucicault (1864)
- *The Red Rover*, Douglas Jerrold (1829)

Handout 28: Extract from *Romeo and Juliet* by William Shakespeare

Setting: Verona, in a public place

Enter SAMPSON and GREGORY, with the swordsmen of the House of Capulet.

SAMPSON: Gregory, on my word, we'll not carry coals.

GREGORY: No, for then we should be colliers.

SAM.: I mean, and we be in choler, we'll draw.

GRE.: Ay, while you live, draw your neck out of collar.

SAM.: I strike quickly, being mov'd.

GRE.: But thou art not quickly mov'd to strike.

SAM.: A dog of the house of Montague moves me.

GRE.: To move is to stir, and to be valiant is to stand; therefore, if thou art mov'd, thou run'st away.

SAM.: A dog of that house shall move me to stand! I will take the wall of any man or maid of Montagues.

Handout 29: Interpreting a dramatic text – key questions

Key questions	What does it mean?
What is the style or genre of the play?	Genre clues:
What do I know about the character or role I am playing or working with?	Clothing/accent/key actions?
What are the key issues when moving from page to stage?	Technical issues: where and what? Time of day? Location?

Handout 30: Extract from *Cyrano de Bergerac* by Edmond Rostand

Extract B

Act 2, Scene 6
Setting: An orchard.

ROXANE: Ofttimes, with hands all bloody from a fall,
You'd run to me! Then—aping mother-ways—
I, in a voice would-be severe, would chide,—

(She takes his hand):

'What is this scratch, again, that I see here?'

(She starts, surprised):

Oh! 'Tis too much! What's this?

(Cyrano tries to draw away his hand):

No, let me see!
At your age, fie! Where did you get that scratch?

CYRANO: I got it—playing at the Porte de Nesle.

ROXANE *(seating herself by the table, and dipping her handkerchief in a glass of water)*:

Give here!

CYRANO *(sitting by her)*:

So soft! So gay maternal-sweet!

ROXANE: And tell me, while I wipe away the blood,
How many 'gainst you?

CYRANO: Oh! A hundred—near.

ROXANE: Come, tell me!

CYRANO: No, let be. But you, come tell
The thing, just now, you dared not . . .

ROXANE *(keeping his hand)*:

Now, I dare!
The scent of those old days emboldens me!
Yes, now I dare. Listen. I am in love.

CYRANO: Ah! . . .

ROXANE: But with one who knows not.

CYRANO: Ah! . . .

ROXANE: Not yet.

CYRANO: Ah! . . .

ROXANE: But who, if he knows not, soon shall learn.

Handout 30: Extract from *Cyrano de Bergerac* by Edmond Rostand (2)

CYRANO: Ah! . . .

ROXANE: A poor youth who all this time has loved
Timidly, from afar, and dares not speak. . .

CYRANO: Ah! . . .

ROXANE: Leave your hand; why, it is fever-hot!—
But I have seen love trembling on his lips.

CYRANO: Ah!. . .

ROXANE *(bandaging his hand with her handkerchief)*:

And to think of it! that he by chance—
Yes, cousin, he is of your regiment!

CYRANO: Ah! . . .

ROXANE *(laughing)*:

—Is cadet in your own company!

CYRANO: Ah!. . .

ROXANE: On his brow he bears the genius-stamp;
He is proud, noble, young, intrepid, fair . . .

CYRANO *(rising suddenly, very pale)*:

Fair!

ROXANE: Why, what ails you?

CYRANO: Nothing; 'tis . . .

(He shows his hand, smiling):

This scratch!

ROXANE: I love him; all is said. But you must know
I have only seen him at the Comedy . . .

CYRANO: How? You have never spoken?

ROXANE: Eyes can speak.

CYRANO: How know you then that he . . .?

ROXANE: Oh! people talk
'Neath the limes in the Place Royale . . .
Gossip's chat
Has let me know . . .

CYRANO: He is a cadet?

ROXANE: In the Guards.

CYRANO: His name?

ROXANE: Baron Christian de Neuvillette.

Handout 31: Monologue comparison table

Tick as many as apply for each monologue.

Monologue	A: Lucy	B: Valere
Contemporary		
Classical		
Verse		
Prose		
Fast pace		
Slow pace		
Comic		
Tragic		
Directed to the audience		
Directed to other characters		

Starting emotion(s): _____

Changing emotion(s): _____

Final emotion(s): _____

Collins Cambridge IGCSE™ Drama Teacher's Guide © HarperCollins *Publishers* 2016   *Permission to photocopy*

Handout 32: Introduction to Stanislavski and 'The System' (1)

Konstantin Stanislavski

Stanislavski (1863–1938) was a theatre performer and director who developed his practice and managed the Moscow Art Theatre. Stanislavki developed 'The System' between 1909 and 1916 as an integrated series of techniques designed to support the actor to systematically develop the capacity to bring dramatic characters and narratives to life. Amongst spectators, suspension of disbelief and maintenance of the fourth wall are considered to be essential outcomes of a successful naturalistic performance. Immersion in The System is intended to help the actor to build absolute belief from the audience in the *reality* of the drama depicted on stage.

Later, between 1934 and 1938, the technique evolved to become a 'method of physical actions' in which emotions are produced through the use of specified actions.

Stanislavski felt that an actor needed to build a life for their character. Using the clues in the text an actor should be able to develop their understanding of the context of the character. The various components of The System are designed to identify the influences that motivate the character to act in particular ways or react to different circumstances or people. The actor works towards building a life *off-stage* to explain what goes on *on-stage*.

Units and Objectives:

One of the more useful aspects of Stanislavski's System is the deconstruction of the text into a series of smaller chunks of action known as units. In each unit, each character then establishes a clear objective for the unit. Usually these objectives are conceived using active verbs – for example, 'To persuade'. Associated verbs can then be translated by the actor into specific actions.

Through-Line and Super-Objective:

Once the text has been divided into a series of units and objectives (which may or may not correspond to the various scenes and acts in a play text), the actor can then establish an overarching objective for the character for the play. For example, for the character of Felix in *Humble Boy* (See Student's Book, Chapter 6, pages 120–133), this could be 'to persuade others of the extent of the loss of my father'. This super-objective can then be attached to a 'through-line' of action for the character, which resembles the graphical reading of a heart beat with the various emotional peaks and troughs annotated on the chart.

Handout 32: Introduction to Stanislavski and 'The System' (2)

Emotion Memory:

An actor can use a personal object that helps them remember a time when they had a very strong feeling close to how their character feels. This can help you re-create the right emotions for your acting. You could also create an emotion memory object [personal prop] for your character to remind them of something that drives or affects their life – for example, a wedding ring for a woman who has recently thrown out her husband after finding he has cheated on her.

'Magic If':

One of Stanislavski's methods for achieving the truthful pursuit of a character's emotion was his 'Magic If'. Actors were required to ask many questions of their characters and themselves. Through the 'Magic If', actors were able to satisfy themselves and their characters' positions of the plot. One of the first questions they had to ask was, 'What if I were in the same situation as my character?' Another variation on this is 'What would I do if I found myself in this (the character's) circumstance?'

The 'Magic If' allowed actors to transcend the confinements of realism by asking them what would occur 'if' circumstances were different, or 'if' the circumstances were to happen to them. By answering these questions as the character, the theatrical actions of the actors would be believable and therefore 'truthful'.

Handout 33: Introduction to Georgian society and theatre (1)

Georgian society and culture

The 'Georgian' period is defined as the period of the reign of the first four Hanoverian kings of Great Britain: George I, George II, George III and George IV. The era covers the period from 1714 to 1830, with a sub-period of the rule of the 'Regent Prince of Wales' (who later became King George IV, from 1820-1830) during the period of mental illness of his father, King George III, from 1811 to 1820.

Georgian **culture** was defined by the works of novelists such as Jane Austen and Henry Fielding and later, the works of the Romantic poets William Blake, John Keats and Percy Shelley. Painters Thomas Gainsborough and Joshua Reynolds captured the aristocracy in their paintings, while John Constable tended to concentrate on the landscape and working people.

In rural areas the **Agricultural Revolution** saw huge changes to the predominance of small communities, as cities began to develop and great swathes of people emigrated to North America to settle the 'new world'. Social reformers brought great change in areas such as the abolition of slavery, prison reform and social justice. Philanthropists began to found hospitals, orphanages and Sunday schools to help the new urban poor. The Georgian period was also a period of rampant imperialism and colonisation with voyages to the Antipodes.

In **architecture**, ornate building projects designed to resemble fashionable shapes of the day, such as the fan, led to the construction of entire terraces of grand houses and public buildings. In the theatre, new buildings were constructed in the 1780s and 1790s and managed by actor managers. Built in 1788, the Georgian Theatre Royal in Richmond, North Yorkshire is the most precise example of an authentic 18th-century playhouse in the UK.

Handout 33: Introduction to Georgian society and theatre (2)

Georgian theatre

Georgian theatre was characterised by great noise and was a fantastically social experience. Audiences were segregated by social class, with the rich seated in the boxes at the side of the stage and the poor squeezed into hot and dusty galleries. Spectators went to be seen as much as to see, and many of the comedies of the later period include use of fans, ornate costumes and props all designed to reflect the fashions of the wealthy patrons and benefactors.

Handout 34: *Humble Boy* characterisation table

Character	Appearance/clothing	Their entrance on stage	Manner / tone of speech
Felix	Overweight, wearing old cricket clothes	'in a stumbling, uncertain way'	
Mercy		Has come to look for Felix (sent by Flora?) but doesn't come too close to him	
Flora	Glamorous, attractive, designer style		

Challenge: Choose one character and make notes on physicality.

Collins Cambridge IGCSE™ Drama Teacher's Guide © HarperCollins *Publishers* 2016   *Permission to photocopy*

Handout 35: *I Love the Daffodils* song

(*Note*: You can find examples of this on You Tube)

I Love the Daffodils

I like the flowers,
I love the daffodils,
I like the mountains,
I love the rolling hills.
I like the fireside
When the lights are high.

bom di ada, bom di ada, bom di ada, bom
bom di ada, bom di ada, bom di ada, bom

I like the flowers,
I love the daffodils,
I like the mountains,
I love the rolling hills.
I like the fireside
When the lights are low.

Handout 36: Characterisation table for Felix

Stage directions and observations	What this might tell us?	Ideas for characterisation: Vocal skills, gesture, proxemics, facial expression, movement
He enters the garden in a 'stumbling, uncertain way'	It might convey the idea of a 'lost' soul, someone who is unsure where to go. Why might this be? Perhaps because of his father's death.	
He is 'transfixed' by the beehive.	The bees were kept by his father, so their removal might seem like another link gone with his father, perhaps even a betrayal?	
He's wearing old, greying cricket clothes, even though it is the day of his father's funeral.		
In the conversation with Mercy, he seems obsessed by the beekeepers who have taken the bees away.		
Even though Mercy tries to encourage him, he ignores her requests to 'come inside'.		
When his mother appears, he speaks to her directly.		
His stammering gets worse when his mother is talking to him.		

Handout 37: Units and objectives for *Humble Boy*

Phase 1 Entrance and looking at beehive before Mercy comes in	Phase 2 Mercy's entrance and their conversation	Phase 3 His mother's entrance and their conversation
Acting ideas The stage directions say he is 'transfixed', so as he enters he must keep his eyes on the hive, drawing the audience's attention to it too. He will take the lid off the hive carefully, gingerly, but not in a fearful way.	**Acting ideas**	**Acting ideas**
Rationale The bees have great meaning to him; they are a link to his father, so the way he takes the lid off should be reverential and done with care.	**Rationale**	**Rationale**

Handout 38: Introduction to 20th-century theatrical realism and Galsworthy (1)

Galsworthy's writing career

- *From the Four Winds*, a collection of short stories, was Galsworthy's first published work in 1897.
- These, and several subsequent works, were published under the pen name John Sinjohn.
- In 1904 John Galsworthy began publishing under his own name.

First Plays

- His first play, *The Silver Box* (1906), became a success, and he followed it up with *The Man of Property* (1906), the first in the *Forsyte* trilogy.

His concern for society

- Galsworthy is known for *The Forsyte Saga*, the first of three trilogies of novels about the eponymous family and connected lives.
- These works dealt with class, and in particular upper-middle class lives.
- Although sympathetic to his characters, he highlights their insular, snobbish and acquisitive attitudes and their suffocating moral codes.

Edwardian literature

- Galsworthy is one of the first writers of the Edwardian era.
- In his works, he challenged some of the ideals of society depicted in the preceding literature of Victorian England.

Recurring themes

- The depiction of a woman in an unhappy marriage illustrates another recurring theme in his work.
- The character of Irene in *The Forsyte Saga* is drawn from Ada Pearson, even though her previous marriage was not as miserable as Irene's.

Social reforms

- Some say that his work is less convincing when it deals with the changing face of wider British society and how it affects people of the lower social classes.
- Through his writings he campaigned for a variety of causes including prison reform, women's rights, and animal welfare, and he opposed censorship.

Handout 38: Introduction to 20th-century theatrical realism and Galsworthy (2)

Selected works by John Galsworthy

- *The Country House* (1907)
- *A Commentary* (1908)
- *Strife* (1909)
- *Fraternity* (1909)
- *The Forsyte Saga* (1906–21)
- *Justice* (1910)
- *The Little Dream* (1911)
- *Escape* (1926)

Features of theatrical realism

- Assertion of the power of the individual to choose.
- Reveals the elements from the real world that highlight the relationships under the surface.
- All aspects of design suggest the real-world setting.

The impact of Galsworthy's plays

- His plays often took up specific social grievances.
- He exposes the double standard of justice as applied to the upper and lower classes in *The Silver Box*.
- He deals with confrontation of capital and labour in *Strife*.
- *Justice,* his most famous play, led to prison reform in England.
- Galsworthy's reaction to the First World War found its expression in *The Mob* (1914), in which the voice of a statesman is drowned in the madness of the war-hungry masses.